Welcome to Free America

Welcome to Free America

David Barker

Free America Immigration Services Press
3722 Ron Paul Avenue
Galtville, von Mises (formerly Indiana)

Printed in Free America, copyright protected by Acme Security.
Copyright 2057 (194 A.F.)

10 9 8 7 6 5 4 3 2 1

Mel's Free America Library Cataloging Data

Barker, David (David R.)
Welcome to Free America/David Barker p. in.
Includes preface and advertisements

ISBN 978-1-105-02779-6

1. International migration--Free America.

2. Free America--Social conditions.

JV6543 .B27 2057 304.873

Original copyright 2011 David Barker. All rights reserved.

Preface

This book is a work of political science fiction. Set in the year 2057, it describes America after government has collapsed. With no government, America's borders are wide open and the economy is booming, so perhaps the biggest transformation the country undergoes is a massive wave of immigration. I have written what is supposed to be a guide for these new immigrants. In capitalist Free America, it will be written for profit, underwritten by companies who want to encourage immigration, and others who want to sell products to new immigrants.

Whether the society I describe is a utopia or a dystopia is up to you, the reader. Economic growth and freedom appeal to most people, but some aspects of a society free of government may be disturbing. My main reason for writing the book, however, is not to debate the merits of government policies or to take a side in political debate, but to imagine what our future might be like. In the increasingly polarized politics of the United States, and in the growing popularity of ideas that were once considered extreme, I see the possibility of dramatic political change as our young century proceeds.

Our current political situation has its roots in the centuries-old debate about the proper size and role of the federal government. The American Revolution itself was a struggle over the size of government. Thomas Jefferson complained in the Declaration of Independence that the King had "sent hither swarms of Officers to harass our people and eat out their substance" and was "imposing taxes upon us without our consent." After independence, Alexander Hamilton wanted a vigorous federal government that would stimulate and direct economic growth, while Thomas Jefferson wanted a small, restrained federal government. Abraham Lincoln and his new Republican Party supported federal subsidies for railroads and other "internal improvements," while southern Democrats wanted to keep federal intrusions to a minimum.

The presidency of Woodrow Wilson and World War I provided advocates of big government an opportunity to realize their dreams. Railroads were nationalized, companies that refused to unionize were seized, a central bank under government control was established, and the top rate of the newly enacted income tax was raised to 77 percent. Republicans during the early and middle 1920s advocated a return to the "normalcy" of small government and low taxes, but by the late 1920s Republican Herbert Hoover was already increasing the role of the federal government, and during the 1930s and 1940s the Great Depression and World War II allowed Democrats to dramatically increase the size and reach of the federal government.

After World War II both parties appeared to accept the new reality of larger government, but Republicans, led by Ronald Reagan, increasingly advocated smaller government. Democrats continued to propose new programs that would expand government. The result resembled a stalemate, with the size of the federal government remaining fairly constant at approximately 20 percent of GDP. Government of this size may be a drag on economic growth, but it certainly isn't enough to stop growth, since income per capita, adjusted for inflation, has nearly quadrupled since World War II.

For many years now, the United States has appeared to be in a sort of equilibrium, with each political party pushing in the opposite direction, but neither making much progress. It is becoming increasingly clear, however, that this equilibrium is not sustainable for long, because both political parties have permitted the country's financial condition to deteriorate. Republicans, while publicly advocating small government and pushing for tax cuts, act like Democrats when it comes to spending. The last time Republicans controlled both houses of congress and the presidency, from 2003-2007, federal spending increased faster than GDP. Democrats, while claiming that they want the rich to pay more in taxes, act like Republicans when it comes to setting up tax breaks for their wealthy friends. While Democrats controlled the government from 2009-2011, federal tax revenue fell faster than GDP. Prominent Democrats have not proposed a major tax increase, even one conditional on economic recovery.

When either party is in opposition their rhetoric becomes more extreme, but they always end up compromising by keeping taxes low and spending high, funding the resulting deficit by borrowing. There are limits to the borrowing capacity of the United States, and when these limits are reached a political crisis seems likely.

Our current equilibrium is something like a long game of tug-of-war over a muddy stream. Eventually, the ground will give way underneath one side or the other, and everyone will end up on the left or the right bank of the stream after a short, messy, and chaotic period where many are dragged through the mud. We already know something about what it will be like if we end up on the left bank. Numerous experiments with government-controlled economies demonstrate the disasters that result from all-powerful states. Human history also shows that mistakes are often repeated, so this outcome remains a possibility.

Less well understood are the results of ending up on the other bank of the stream. Those in the United States who oppose big government are not fascists, monarchists, or theocrats—they are increasingly libertarian. If they win, what will America be like? There has never been a modern society with minimal government, so we really don't know. Even those who advocate reducing the size of government rarely express what they think the ideal size of government is, or how we would know when to stop cutting taxes and government services.

An economic or constitutional crisis in America could seriously undermine the perceived legitimacy of government, swinging American politics in a libertarian direction. We don't know how far the momentum of such a movement would take the country, or what the results would be if it succeeded completely.

This book is an early attempt to answer these questions. As an economist and entrepreneur, I have tried to think about the effect of broad economic forces, and the results of actions of opportunistic business people. The society I describe will shock some people and excite others. Like any economic and political system, it has advantages and disadvantages. Personally, I find it infinitely preferable to the other extreme of totalitarian government, but for selfish reasons I have mixed feelings about whether I would choose it over our present system. My real estate business benefits from government regulations that restrict competition, such as zoning and building codes. Real estate is treated better than other businesses under the tax code, so I probably receive more in government benefits than I pay in taxes. I also wonder whether unrestricted immigration would eventually cause me to feel like an alien in my home country. I am convinced, however, that for society as a whole the benefits of eliminating government would greatly exceed the costs.

But whether we prefer it or not is immaterial. Political and economic forces are often beyond the ability of voters or leaders to stop. Considering alternate futures is important, not because we have any choice about the direction of human society, but so that we might mentally and physically prepare for what may lie ahead.

I used one stylistic change to illustrate the prevailing attitude toward government in the year 2051 – the names of government offices and political parties are not capitalized. In Free America in 2051, government is not respected, whether it is encountered in foreign countries or in American history. Use of the lower case is a subtle but powerful way to register contempt, just as leftist scholars began using the lower case for the word "president" around 1970 to indicate their dislike of president Richard Nixon.

Acknowledgments

I thank Jan Lester and David McDonough for educating me about libertarianism at the London School of Economics nearly thirty years ago and for continuing to do so. I also thank David Steele and Ray Percival for helping me to sharpen my ideas, and David Friedman for writing *The Machinery of Freedom*. I owe a huge debt to the Department of Economics and Booth School of Business at the University of Chicago, particularly Sam Peltzman, Robert Lucas, Gary Becker, George Stigler, Robert Aliber, George Tolley, and Andrei Shleifer. I learned as much from my fellow graduate students in those days as I did from my professors, and I thank them for being such good friends. My business colleagues, partners, and employees have taught me more than they know. I am grateful to the finance department of the University of Iowa for providing me with an academic home for the past fifteen years. Finally I thank my wife, children, brother, sisters, parents, aunts, uncles, cousins, and friends for putting up with many years of political arguments.

Welcome to Free America!

You are a part of the greatest experiment in human history—a society with rules, but no rulers. America has no government, and that is probably why you have come. Anticipating that you might find Free America confusing at first, we designed this guidebook to help you understand the basics of daily life in your new homeland. Because the history of Free America is misrepresented in government-controlled countries, we also give you an honest account of the collapse of the united states government and the development of this new kind of society.

One of the most common misconceptions about Free America is that it is a society without rules. Nothing could be further from the truth! Those who endanger others or their property face serious consequences. Too many early immigrants failed to understand their responsibilities; they and Free America paid a heavy price. Today, however, with the help of private protection and insurance contracts, life in Free America can be safer and more secure than anywhere else in the world.

The tremendous opportunities available in Free America are no misconception. As has been the case for centuries, immigrants come to America for both economic and spiritual reasons. If you have come for economic opportunities, you will find that our economy is booming and great wealth is attainable. If you have come for spiritual growth, you will be amazed at the number and variety of communities that will welcome you. Perhaps you simply want to live in a truly free country, where you can say, read, and write what you please, raise your children as you see fit, engage in any recreation that you enjoy, take risks, protect yourself as you choose, and conduct your business free from the prying eyes and grasping hands of others. If you yearn to breathe free, as the Statue of Liberty promises, coming to Free America was the right choice.

We appreciate your purchase of this guide and encourage you to patronize our advertisers, who have purchased space at the end of this book.

Contents

1. A Short History of Free America 1
2. What to Do First 13
3. Finding a Job 17
4. Where to Live 23
5. Protecting Yourself... 31
6. Punishment of Crimes 45
7. Money 49
8. Getting Around 55
9. Health and Medical Care 59
10. Intellectual Property 63
11. Children 67
12. Drugs, Prostitution, Gambling, and Guns 71
13. The Environment and Energy Use 75
14. The Economy.. 81
15. Relations with Other Countries 89
16. The Future of Free America 91

1
A Short History of Free America

The united states of America (Free Americans no longer capitalize "united states" or government titles) was an independent constitutional republic from 1776 to 2031. A series of fiscal and constitutional crises beginning in 2016 weakened and eventually caused the collapse of the national and local governments, resulting in the birth of Free America. The central cause of the government's final collapse was its simple inability to pay its employees, contractors, and debtors.

For over 150 years of American history, the size and scope of government was small. Taxes were low and government intrusion into most aspects of the economy and society was limited. The combination of the Great Depression and World War II, however, caused an unprecedented expansion of government activity. Taxes increased, and government spending increased even more, causing the national debt to balloon to 120 percent of the GDP. Taxes and spending remained high, but fell into balance after World War II, allowing the federal debt to steadily decline to 32 percent of the GDP during the presidency of Jimmy Carter in the 1970s.

The pressure to lower taxes that began during the Carter administration mounted in the 1980s during Ronald Reagan's presidency. Tax rates fell, but there was no corresponding political pressure to cut government spending. In the first full year of the Reagan administration, government debt as a fraction of the GDP began an increase that would continue, with few interruptions, until the final collapse of the united states government.

By the late twentieth century, the contradictory demands of American voters for both low taxes and expensive government services had become a clear pattern. The defeat of president George H. W. Bush in 1992 and the loss of control of congress by president William Clinton in 1994, both following unpopular tax increases, convinced the two major political parties, the republicans and the democrats, that major tax increases would endanger their electoral prospects. As a result, tax rates for most Americans remained below those of the mid-twentieth century. Attempts to increase taxes between 2010 and 2020 again resulted in election defeats, causing more members of congress from both parties to sign "tax pledges" promising not to raise taxes under any circumstances.

Federal government spending, however, continued to increase faster than other sectors of the economy. Periodic attempts to cut spending met the same reaction from voters as the tax increases. Economic weakness and high unemployment began in 2001, and after the Panic of 2008, many economists claimed that additional government spending was necessary in order to avoid catastrophic levels of unemployment, giving voters intellectual justification for their support of unsustainable economic policies.

Under normal circumstances, the federal government had three basic methods of financing its activities: it could tax, borrow, or create money. Taxation, as older people and immigrants from other countries will recall, is the theft of money and property from citizens and businesses by a government. Government borrowing was cheap as long as investors had confidence in the ultimate ability of governments to obtain tax revenue, but when that confidence collapsed, borrowing became much more expensive. The third alternative for the government was to create money simply by printing it or by producing it through accounting entries. Over time, all three of these alternatives became unavailable, and the government was unable to pay its bills.

At first, the federal government borrowed to finance its growing deficit, but political discontent with the high federal debt levels grew. In 2018, a group of politicians resurrected the reform party that Ross Perot created in 1992 and won several seats in congress. The party's main issue was the federal debt, just as it had been for Perot, but this time, they advocated a partial repudiation of the government debt. Their reasoning was that a default would make it harder for the federal government to borrow, making a repeat of the current situation difficult, and would allow the savings in interest to be used for tax relief, helping the economy.

The electoral success of the reform party, modest as it was, caused many investors in government bonds to lose confidence that they would be repaid, and higher promised interest rates became necessary to sell the growing number of bonds the government was offering. Investor concern spread to banks and businesses that held government debt, increasing their borrowing costs. As these higher rates came to be reflected in business and consumer borrowing rates, the economy weakened even more. Rising unemployment led to demands for more government spending, resulting in more debt, creating a vicious circle. Interest rates and debt eventually increased to levels that would cause a political crisis.

The crisis culminated in a 2021 vote on whether to raise the federal debt ceiling. Without an increase, the federal government was legally prohibited from borrowing additional funds. Congress eventually passed the increase by a single vote, but the newly elected reform party president Sarah Palin vetoed the measure, and congress was unable to override her veto.

Since further borrowing was impossible, and because there was no political will to raise taxes, which would, in any event, have worsened the economic situation, calls to print money to pay off creditors became more common. A new populist movement took the unlikely figure of William Jennings Bryan as its hero, and adopted his slogan, "Shall the People Rule?" Bryan's opposition to the teaching of the theory of evolution made him popular with right-wing movements. Moreover, accounts of his advocacy of inflationary expansion of the money supply resonated with the many people recently bankrupted by high levels of debt and falling incomes. Memories of 1970s era inflation had faded so completely that politicians who warned of the dangers of excessive money creation lost in the 2022 congressional elections by landslide margins.

When president Palin delivered her famous rendition of portions of Bryan's "Cross of Gold" speech in 2023, foreign investors in united states debt panicked, and interest rates skyrocketed. Business investment collapsed, and unemployment reached 30 percent. Subsequently, president Palin's popularity dropped, and a "hard money" political movement developed, leading to a new congress that passed strict controls on the ability of the federal reserve and the united states treasury to expand the money supply.

Due both to the weak economy and increasing tax evasion, federal and local government tax receipts fell dramatically. Attempts to increase the funding of the internal revenue service were blocked in congress, and militia threats against IRS agents hurt the ability of the agency to recruit new employees.

Unable to borrow, raise taxes, or print money, the federal government began cutting some spending programs. One of the first to be cut was aid to state and local governments amounting to more than one quarter of their revenue, forcing these already weakened governments to confront their desperate budgetary situations. State constitutions prohibited them from running budget deficits, and both the state and local governments were unable to gather political support for bond issues, which would have been extremely difficult to sell even if they had been authorized. State and local governments also faced strong political movements against tax increases.

To close their budget gaps, state and local governments slashed their budgets for schools, highways, prisons, and police. Many state employees were laid off and others went on strike. Crime quickly increased. Particularly terrifying to many people was the growth of highway robbery. The robberies began with stolen patrol cars and the impersonation of police officers, but motorists soon learned to ignore flashing lights and sirens, making the highways even more lawless than they had already been. Robbers then began blocking highways with trucks, robbing the backed up cars, and escaping by driving ahead of their makeshift roadblocks, dropping land mines behind them to prevent pursuit. Many robbers turned out to be veterans of the wars in Iraq and Afghanistan, where they had learned a great deal about improvised explosive devices.

After a freak snowstorm closed unplowed roads for two weeks throughout the Deep South, bandits took the opportunity to stockpile equipment and ammunition at strategic locations and took complete control of some stretches of interstate highways. Following a particularly brutal series of highway robberies, a group of laid-off highway patrolmen and local business leaders in Mississippi took control of the 212-mile segment of Interstate 55 between Memphis, Tennessee, and Jackson, Mississippi. After dozens of robbers were killed and hung on roadside light poles as warnings, the robberies stopped. The group charged tolls, cleared snow, and made road repairs. Their popularity convinced the Mississippi state government to allow them to retain control, particularly since Interstate 55 was the only reliable land route for government officials to leave the state capitol. The group made enormous profits, and other groups prepared to do the same in other parts of the country.

The success of the Interstate 55 group sparked movements in three states for constitutional conventions that would disband their state governments, sell state property, and use the money to pay off creditors. The leftover money was then to be distributed to taxpayers in proportion to the tax payments they had made over the past five years. When the movements succeeded in Mississippi and Oklahoma in 2027, however, the federal government found the states to be in violation of article 4, section 4 of the constitution, which required the united states to guarantee to each state a republican form of government, and declared the two states to be in a state of rebellion.

The brutality and efficiency of the federal invasions of Mississippi and Oklahoma shocked the country. Every delegate to the state constitutional conventions and every member of the state legislatures of these two states disappeared. Sympathetic journalists and business leaders also vanished. Army tanks took positions at most highway intersections, and soldiers established checkpoints outside all cities and towns. The leaders of the Interstate 55 group were arrested and charged with numerous federal crimes. As some of the bandits they killed when combating the highway robberies were black, the charges against them included murder motivated by racial hatred, a federal crime punishable by death. Fifteen members of the group were imprisoned, and five were publicly executed. Marches and demonstrations were banned, and the few that were attempted were fired on and dispersed by federal troops.

There was a period of quiet after the invasions of Mississippi and Oklahoma. Federal authorities established new state governments, and held elections, although boycotts kept vote totals very low. Economic activity suffered nationwide as investment capital flowed out of the united states to more politically stable countries.

Continued high unemployment hardened attitudes against tax increases, and also increased calls for additional spending to "stimulate" the economy. Federal authorities worried that continuing to cut spending on programs like social security, medicare, and veteran's benefits would hurt their popularity even more than the invasions had done, so to raise cash to support spending, they began to sell federal assets. Post offices and federal office buildings around the country were sold first, followed by large tracts of federal land and oil and mineral rights in western states. These sales kept the government afloat, but it became increasingly clear over time that spending levels were unsustainable.

A new political movement formed to call a constitutional convention to change the relationship between the states and the federal government, and the required number of thirty-four states eventually passed calls for a convention. The 2029 convention proved to be an unruly affair, with rival groups from several states demanding to be seated, and numerous terrorist threats causing the gathering to be interrupted and moved several times. Rumors of paramilitary groups threatening to kill delegates who "sold out" proved later to have been unfounded, but they raised the level of tension considerably. None of the constitutional amendments passed by the convention were able to pass by the required three-quarters of the state legislatures, so they did not become law. The failure of the convention further undermined confidence in the federal government to solve the economic problems of the country.

Accounts of investors receiving "sweetheart deals" when federal assets were auctioned created a new political crisis, and put a temporary halt to asset sales. Unable to raise cash by any means, the federal government again slashed spending. In 2031, all federal outlays, salaries, payments to contractors, purchases of goods, and payments to debtors and social security recipients were reduced by one-third.

A massive strike by public employee unions protesting the cuts quickly ground most government operations to a halt. Social security recipients marched on Washington, creating even more chaos, and private contractors, on whom the government had come to rely for many vital functions, began shutting down their operations. At the same time, a peace movement against the long-running war in Iran gained ground, and a series of mutinies by underequipped troops forced the abandonment of the war and the sudden return of large numbers of soldiers to the united states. Many of these soldiers were unable to find employment and joined the demonstrators in Washington, increasing the instability of the situation.

Due to both economic and political pressures, the occupation of Mississippi and Oklahoma ended in 2032. The state governments that were set up by the retreating federal authorities quickly collapsed, and most of the remaining state property was auctioned, although a shell state government with no real authority was maintained to avoid another confrontation with the federal government. As entrepreneurs found ways to operate formerly government functions for a profit, prices of state assets rose, and other states and local governments began auctioning their property to pay debts and their remaining state employees.

Attracted by rising asset prices, the federal government rejoined the process of auctioning assets in 2034. By this time, however, asset prices were rising because of falling confidence in the united states dollar. Rumors of secret and illegal printing of currency abounded, and many investors saw the auctions as the only way to unload dollars for a reasonable return.

By 2037, annual inflation had reached 25 percent. A growing number of businesses refused to accept dollars, opting for foreign currencies instead. Disgruntled Iran War veterans rioted over receiving their long-overdue back pay in depreciating dollars and over rumors that foreigners were buying government assets at auctions. A series of anti-foreign-trade laws was passed, further weakening the economy. A wave of general strikes supported by war veterans caused chaos in many cities.

Panicked over the prospect of rioting soldiers joining striking workers to topple the federal government, the president declared martial law in 2039. Soldiers sent to subdue rioters joined them instead and marched on the White House. Dozens of secret service agents were killed in a short clash, and soon afterward secret service agents around the country were arrested and detained by army soldiers. In a few cases, when state police forces challenged army units, claiming they were violating the *posse comitatus* act, army soldiers disguised themselves as members of the coast guard, which was exempt from the act.

A shadowy independent army unit assumed responsibility for White House security. Congress impeached and convicted the president for illegally declaring martial law, just minutes after the vice president was mysteriously killed while inspecting White House defenses. The speaker of the house claimed the presidency, but because she was rumored to have been born in Canada and could not prove otherwise, aides to the president of the senate declared that the speaker was constitutionally ineligible and claimed the presidency for their boss, although he was 102 years old. In a widely viewed press conference, the secretary of state, next in line for the presidency, attempted to manipulate the confused president of the senate into admitting that he was unable to carry out the duties of the presidency. A brawl broke out between the staffs of the two men. Congress promptly impeached and removed the secretary of state from office, and two days later the 102-year-old president suffered a stroke. A meeting of seven cabinet officers invoked the 25th amendment to the constitution and declared the president to be unfit, and the secretary of the treasury claimed the presidency. The senate quickly named a new president pro tempore, who claimed that he should be sworn in as president, although supporters of the bedridden former president pro tempore of the senate claimed that the meeting to declare him unfit was illegal, because a majority of the cabinet was not present. The secretary of the treasury countered the senate's move by claiming that the presidential succession act was unconstitutional, quoting former president James Madison as saying that the constitution only permitted executive branch officers to succeed to the presidency.

The response of congress was to impeach all cabinet secretaries and all of the undersecretaries who had been confirmed by the senate. The secretary of the treasury, however, claimed that he was already president, and could only be removed if the chief justice of the supreme court presided over his trial in the senate. The chief justice happened to be the secretary's brother-in-law, and announced that he would refuse to preside over such a trial, even if the senate was willing to declare the secretary president in order to remove him.

Further complicating matters, the house of representatives named a new speaker, who also claimed the presidency, and the secretary of defense constructed a complicated legal argument, based on the wild sequence of events, that the secretary of the treasury had been legally removed by the senate, and that the secretary of defense had automatically succeeded to the presidency, and also could not be removed without the chief justice presiding over a trial. Rumors flew that the secretary of defense had organized a renegade group of military officers to assassinate the chief justice so that one of his allies would become chief justice and refuse to preside over his trial.

Four members of the supreme court went into hiding, worried about rumors of plots against them by the secretary of defense. With a quorum impossible, the court refused to meet to decide the matter. Even if it had met, many members of congress declared that the supreme court had no jurisdiction over the matter, and it was unclear whether any decision it made would have been respected.

Faced with five powerful claimants to the presidency, each with plausible constitutional arguments, the joint chiefs of staff declared that they did not know who the legitimate president was, and assumed the role of commander in chief of the armed forces for themselves.

The short-lived military government destroyed the remaining value of the dollar by printing money to pay soldiers, military contractors, and other government obligations. The combination of lower economic activity due to the strikes and uncertainty and the increased supply of money caused inflation to accelerate, and it eventually reached levels of thousands of percent per month. As businesses and foreign governments increasingly refused payment in dollars, most remaining federal employees deserted their jobs. Except for parts of the military, the federal government ceased to function. Some military units supported themselves by collecting taxes at gunpoint from large businesses and wealthy citizens. The gold they collected was used to hold what remained of the military together.

By 2040, every bank in the united states was insolvent. The dollar was abandoned as a usable currency. Savings held in cash or dollar-denominated bonds became worthless. Insurance policies that promised payment in dollars were also worthless, and those who lost property to fire and theft were wiped out. Gold mining and trading companies, some of which had purchased huge quantities of gold from the government at auction, began issuing gold certificates that soon circulated as currency throughout the country.

In 2041, Mexico began moving troops into southern Texas, New Mexico, and Arizona on the pretext of protecting Mexican nationals from anti-foreigner riots. Canada also mobilized troops along its border with the united states on the pretext of protecting itself from American bandits. The real motivation of both countries was territorial expansion at the expense of the united states. Sensing opportunity, China and the European Union both offered assistance to Canada and Mexico. Russia launched a small amphibious assault on an uninhabited area of the Alaskan coast, and Japan sent a fleet of ships to Hawaii.

To combat the threat of foreign invasion, a group of the largest businesses in the united states made a secret offer to the joint chiefs of staff: they would finance military operations, preventing a collapse of the armed forces, in return for control of the military. The group offered large payments in gold to the top military officers, and they eventually accepted the offer. Once controlled by the business council, the joint chiefs quickly ordered nuclear warning strikes on uninhabited areas of the Mexican desert, Russian Siberia, the Canadian north, and a Japanese island. All of these countries quickly withdrew their forces. The arrangement between the business and military leaders was made public, and they quickly became national heroes. They then announced the final liquidation of the federal government, and Army soldiers evicted the remaining members of congress from the capital building and Washington, DC. All remaining federal property was auctioned, with payments required to be in gold, and the receipts were distributed to taxpayers in proportion to their tax payments for the past five years.

Foreign invasion was no longer a threat, but foreign countries continued their attempts to influence events in America. In 2042, a group of former united states government officials was arrested for war crimes while traveling abroad. The group included former presidents William Clinton, age 95, George W. Bush, age 95, and Barack Obama, age 80. Clinton was arrested on charges related to bombings in Serbia over a half century earlier, Bush on charges related to the beginning of the Iraq War, and Obama on charges related to drone attacks on several countries during his presidency. To the surprise of the foreign governments arresting them, Americans were mostly indifferent to the fate of their former presidents. None of them were able to raise sufficient funds for an adequate legal defense. Clinton and Bush died in prison in The Hague. Obama was eventually released, but angry about the lack of support he received from America, he retired to Indonesia.

By 2043, the last remaining state and local governments collapsed, as taxpayers refused to pay their tax bills in gold certificates. In some cities, an orderly auction process had led to private ownership of streets, and private security firms, often owned by former police officials, kept order. In other cities, ownership was unclear and crime rates soared. Immigrants poured into the country, which by this time had no border security; many of them were newly released prisoners from other countries. These countries hoped both to save money on prisoner maintenance and to destabilize the former united states of America.

The situation went from bad to worse in 2044 with a run on Old Gold, the largest gold certificate-issuing company. It quickly became clear that the company had issued far more certificates than it had in gold. Observers around the world expected the former united states to descend quickly into complete anarchy and chaos.

What happened instead was the beginning of a slow process of free market institution-building. Successful owner-operators of streets in stable cities took over operations in other cities, sometimes by voluntary agreement of property-owners along streets, and sometimes by force. Local private security companies began offering increasingly complex protection contracts. The lynching of Old Gold executives in New York City's Battery Park convinced financial companies of their need for additional protection, and security companies offered to provide it in return for the financial companies' agreement to follow a set of regulations.

In response to the wave of criminal immigrants, most communities established checkpoints and forbade the entry of anyone who was unable to prove united states citizenship before its collapse. Seeing the opportunity to profit from the demand for labor in some rapidly growing areas of the country, groups of investors set up immigrant centers, some attached to newly purchased airports, and some to shipping ports. Demand for immigrant labor eventually caused most neighborhoods and cities to accept immigrants, but many others remain closed.

As protection firms consolidated and grew in sophistication, they began to share data and establish databases of biometric information and criminal offenses. The worst criminals from the early immigration waves found that they were unable to obtain protection and were hunted down and sold to incarceration companies.

By 2049, violent crime was nearly eliminated in most cities, the value of gold and other commodity-backed certificates had stabilized, and visible unemployment and homelessness were eliminated. During the depths of the crises of the 2020s and 2030s, minimum wage laws were still enforced, creating huge numbers of unemployed people who roamed about cities, often committing crimes. Building codes were also enforced, making it difficult to construct affordable housing, which meant that homeless people had been very visible in every city. As enforcement of these and other regulations collapsed, the unemployed found low-wage jobs, and entrepreneurs constructed cheap housing.

The nuclear strikes of 2041 proved a powerful deterrent to foreign invasion. When internal and external security reached levels acceptable to most Americans, they began to accept the new system.

For a time, upside-down Stars and Stripes flags were commonly flown as a statement that the country was in distress and that the new state of affairs was illegal. Over time, these flags and the right-side-up version largely disappeared and were replaced by several popular banners, including the Gadsden "Don't Tread on Me" flag, flags with rainbows and flowers, Christian flags, yin-yang flags, and many others.

The term "Free America" is now the most common name for the area that used to be controlled by the government of the united states of America.

2

What to Do First

You may be reading this book on a plane or ship on your way to Free America, wondering what you will do when you arrive. Of course, there will be no immigration check, no passport stamp, and no customs examination. Before leaving the immigrant complex where you arrive, however, if you haven't already done so, you will need to arrange for basic services such as a protection contract and health insurance.

Unless you already have a protection contract, it is not a good idea to land in Free America outside of an immigrant complex. You could be picked up and sent to an incarceration facility, and arranging for protection from there can be difficult. Immigration complexes provide everything you need for a safe and easy transition into a new life in Free America.

Obtaining a protection contract should not be a problem, since you probably received a biometric check before you were allowed to board your ship or airplane to travel to Free America. Transportation companies perform these checks to find matches in criminal and debtor databases. Travelers matching these entries are turned over to the protection firm with a contract for their capture, after which the airline or shipping company collects a bounty. The protection firm then incarcerates or returns these travelers to their country of origin. Once you are in Free America, you will appreciate these checks, for they are an important reason why crime is low and businesses are profitable. Profits that transportation companies earn from the capture of individuals wanted by protection firms also help to keep transportation fares low.

Since you have passed the biometric check, as soon as you arrive, you will be as much a legitimate part of Free America as anyone else. Free America has no immigration quotas and no citizenship requirements; everyone has the same right to live, work, and invest here.

The immigrant complex is attached to the airport or shipping port where you will disembark, and contains a number of hotels, restaurants, and other businesses. The complex has been designed with immigrants in mind. You will find everything from Japanese-style capsule hotels to luxury resorts within walking distance. If you have no money, work is always available within the complex, but the pay is very low. If you choose to make beds, sweep floors, or wash dishes, you will barely earn enough to pay for your food and very rough sleeping accommodations. Many employers offer their own food and lodging, and some offer only food and lodging, with no additional pay. Businesses with a "Hiring" sign in the window will usually hire on the spot. Remember that employees without contracts can be fired immediately for any reason, and contract employment within immigrant complexes is difficult to obtain.

Criminal activity within immigrant complexes has nearly been eliminated. Complexes compete with each other for immigrant traffic, and early reports of criminal activity led to the bankruptcy of several transportation companies, as immigrants chose to travel to safer facilities. Security cameras are everywhere, and security guards respond quickly to any signs of trouble. Immigrants accused of crimes who have not obtained protection contracts (see chapter 5) will be sent back to their home countries if they are lucky, and sold to incarceration facilities otherwise.

Contrary to what you may have read, food at immigrant complex restaurants is safe to eat. If you are concerned, look for the "FACE" (Free America Clean Eatery) sign on the door. The FACE certification process is rigorous, and those restaurants that pass it can be trusted. A rash of counterfeit FACE signs was eliminated a few years ago, and the offending restaurant owners were severely punished. Protection firms for restaurants do not require FACE membership, but they do not provide protection from the FACE organization for restaurants who counterfeit FACE signs. Even restaurants without a FACE or other certification are usually clean and safe, however, since news of poor food or service spreads quickly on the Internet.

The business and shopping areas of the immigrant complex will contain offices of agencies that help new immigrants find work and arrange transportation. Depending on your level of skill and experience, different options will be available to you. Unskilled laborers will usually need to sign contracts requiring them to work for a specified length of time, often five years. If you sign such a contract, you will be offered immediate transportation to a worksite. There, you will receive food and lodging and be given a choice about how to receive your pay: a lump sum payment at the end of your five-year term, or smaller monthly or annual payments to you or remitted to relatives abroad. You should take your time in signing an employment contract, for there are many employers competing for workers, and they offer a variety of terms and conditions. Of course, you will also need to choose a protection firm to enforce your employment contract.

Your freedom to choose your employment will depend on how you have financed your journey. Many companies offer transportation to immigrants on credit, on the condition that employment in a specified field is obtained immediately upon arrival. Some repayment contracts are straight debt, with regular monthly payments owed, while others give transportation companies a share of your future income for a specified length of time, or even for your lifetime. If you have a repayment contract with a transportation company, you will not be allowed to leave the immigrant complex until you have found employment. Many immigrants now sell shares of their future income on a stock exchange in order to repay their transportation loan; this can be done from within the immigrant complex.

Before you leave the immigrant complex, it is important that you obtain a protection contract and medical insurance. Protection and very basic medical care are provided for free within the immigrant complex, but outside of the complex, neither of these is guaranteed without contracts with appropriate firms.

3

Finding a Job

Jobs are plentiful in Free America. If you walk down any street, you will see "Hiring" signs in windows, and if you search the Internet by neighborhood, you will find many individuals and businesses trying to fill positions. You are free to work for anyone, under any terms upon which you and your employer agree. There is no minimum wage and no guarantee of holidays, sick days, or overtime pay. Employment is often very informal; anyone needing assistance with a business or household might simply offer a person on the street cash in return for performing a task, and no paperwork or even exchange of identities is required.

Employers can hire and fire employees lacking a contract at will. Employees are free to attempt to negotiate contracts with employers, however, and those with skills in demand are often able to obtain very generous pay and time off. These contracts can be enforced by protection firms.

Wages

While it is true that wages for jobs that do not require extensive skills are low, the cost of living in Free America is also quite low. There are no taxes, and rent and food costs can be very low. Unskilled workers usually find that their standard of living in Free America is far higher than it was at home, which is why so many of them keep coming. Many are able to achieve an acceptable standard of living while sending most of their pay home to relatives. For those who are interested only in quickly saving as much money as possible, low quality housing that would not be permitted in other developed countries is available at very low rents.

Skilled workers in many fields are often in short supply and high demand in Free America, and employment terms for these workers can be very generous. Companies currently offer high pay and generous vacation allowances to trained engineers, lawyers, aircraft pilots, salespeople, and many other specialists. Workers with training and experience in fields like these can often negotiate long-term contracts with no obligation to work beyond a single year.

The line between employee and entrepreneur is less clear in Free America than it is in other places. You might provide services to several businesses and negotiate employment contracts with each one. You might work part-time or from a distance. Your contract might give you a share of the profits of the company you work for, or the option to convert a fixed salary into ownership in the future. A growing number of people are coming to think of themselves as business owners, with their own skills as the primary asset of the business, instead of as an employee, and many of them sell shares of their future income on publicly traded stock markets.

Potential profit for entrepreneurially minded workers in Free America is unlimited. Many immigrants begin as unskilled laborers and become very wealthy. Of course, the risks of business ventures are considerable, and many workers prefer the security of long-term employment contracts with a single employer.

Unions

Employees are free to form unions, but if they strike or threaten other actions against their employer, they can be fired. In fact, an employer can fire employees for forming or even assembling just to discuss forming a union if he or she chooses. If workers occupy company property or picket on a sidewalk without the sidewalk owner's permission, they can be prosecuted for trespass. Due to the large number of immigrants entering Free America, wages for unskilled work are very low and employers usually have no difficulty replacing workers.

Some formerly government protected labor unions have reinvented themselves as labor providers. The International Brotherhood of Teamsters, for example, provides daily, weekly, monthly, yearly, or longer-term labor to a variety of businesses, and negotiates the laborers' pay and working conditions. Clients use the Teamsters to recruit and sort workers and certify their quality. Contract negotiations do not lead to strikes, however, because employers are able to choose from a variety of labor providers. The resources of protection firms far exceed those of labor providers, and so any attempt to intimidate employers into using their services would be futile.

Contractual Employment

Contractual employment is common in Free America. Skilled workers and even unskilled workers who prove themselves loyal and reliable may be offered long-term employment contracts. In some cases, employers simply offer to guarantee employment at a certain wage for some length of time, subject to employee performance, but usually, the employee is also under certain obligations. Typical contracts require employees to work for one to five years. Some contracts can be broken with a monetary payment, others can be broken only if a substitute employee is offered, and others cannot be broken at all without severe penalties such as incarceration in private prisons.

Any employment contract should be reviewed with a representative of your protection firm. They will explain the terms of the contract and what protection they can provide. Remember that your protection firm will not help you violate the terms of your contract. If you freely agree to a provision, even if it is something that your protection contract is supposed to guard against, your employment contract will take precedence. Suppose, for example, that your protection contract promises to obtain restitution and punishment in case a negligent act results in personal injury, but your employment contract releases your employer from liability for injury. In this case, your protection contract will not help you if you are injured on the job, even if your employer's negligence has caused the injury.

An employee with a long-term contract who leaves without the employer's permission or without paying the contract termination fee will be subject to prosecution. Protection firms of employers often have the responsibility of tracking down runaway employees, extracting restitution or incarcerating the offenders when they are found. An employee's protection firm can similarly pursue an employer who fails to live up to the terms of an employment contract. Contracts are typically recorded by the protection firms of both employer and employee, often with a neutral adjudication firm specified in case of disputes.

Many immigrants have been brought to Free America under long-term or even lifetime employment contracts, only to escape from their employers. Enclaves of escaped employees exist in remote areas, and their capture by employer protection firms has proven highly controversial. Employment contracts of five years or less are generally accepted as legitimate, but many people and businesses have boycotted protection firms that enforce longer-term employment contracts. As a result, the cost of protection contracts for employers using long-term contracts has risen significantly. This cost increase and the low cost of immigrant labor have reduced the use of long-term employee obligations, particularly those over ten years.

For immigrants who are concerned about the treatment of employees with long-term contracts, it is important to remember that there are voluntary agreements. Work is available under shorter terms or under no continuing obligation at all.

Employment Disputes

Disputes between employers and employees are common, but they are now usually adjudicated very efficiently. For example, suppose that an employee has a five-year contract to work for a specified wage subject to good performance. The employer fires the employee for bad performance, but the employee maintains that his or her performance has been good. The employee's protection firm and the employer's protection firm will review the evidence and attempt a resolution. If they cannot reach an agreement, they will appeal to an arbitration firm that would have been selected by the protection firms in advance. The arbitration firm's decision in the matter is usually final. Protection firms have conflicting incentives when they decide whether to appeal a case to an arbitration firm. Arbitration is expensive, and constant demands for arbitration can damage a relationship between protection firms. On the other hand, demanding arbitration convinces clients that the protection firm will stand up for them, and can help to recruit and retain clients.

Some protection firms require jury trials in cases of dispute with an employer, but clients of these firms usually have a difficult time finding employment.

Income Securitization

Income securitization essentially means selling shares in your future income. Millions of Free Americans have sold some percentage of their income in public markets, either for a fixed period of time or for their lifetime. Shares of their income are heavily traded and are often aggregated into mutual funds, allowing investors to own shares of thousands of people at once. Income securitization is helpful for financing an education, the purchase of a house or car, or to raise money for a business venture or an uninsured medical procedure.

Income securitization brokerage firms have offices throughout Free America and can be contacted over the Internet. A brokerage firm will assess your skills through a battery of knowledge and intelligence tests and gather documentation about your work and education history. They will also ask you about your future employment and business plans. Then they will summarize this information and distribute it to financial institutions for bids. When you receive the bids, usually within two to three days, you can decide how many shares to sell, or whether to sell shares at all.

Suppose, for example, that you hope to earn $40,000 per year as a computer consultant to a variety of firms, and as you gain experience, you believe that your income will grow. You might receive a bid of $7,000 for each percentage point of your future income for life, with few conditions placed on your activities and employment choices, and another bid of $500,000 for a 51 percent share of your income with strict conditions attached.

If you choose to sell, say, 10 percent of your income for $70,000, you will have a great deal of choice about where and for whom to work. If you are unemployed or underemployed for a prolonged period of time, your investors will have the option of hiring an employment agency to find a suitable offer of employment for you. If you decline the offer, your investors will have a variety of options, depending on their contract with you. Typically, investors have the right to incarcerate a person who refuses reasonable offers of employment for as long as it takes for the investors to receive a specified amount.

Investors purchasing larger shares, typically 51 percent and above, usually require more control over the lives of the people they are investing in. Electronic monitoring prevents movement away from an employer or place of business, employers submit regular reports on performance, and any changes of employment or business must be approved by the investors.

Of course, since income shares are traded on public markets, individuals are free to repurchase shares in themselves. Many employees and businesspeople sell substantial shares in their income when they are young, hoping to earn enough to repurchase all outstanding shares before they retire.

4

Where to Live

The variety of communities in Free America is truly staggering. There are towns and neighborhoods that define themselves by religion, sexual preferences, child rearing practices, philosophical beliefs, race, ethnicity, and intelligence. There are also many diverse neighborhoods containing a wide variety of immigrants and native-born Americans. But what most new arrivals find most surprising about Free America is the increasingly specialized nature of many of its communities. The collapse of local governments in the 2040s caused severe disruptions in many cities and towns, but they are reinventing themselves in surprising ways. Many are more vibrant and prosperous than ever, but they differ in interesting respects.

The Development of Free American Cities

As local governments declined during the 2030s and 2040s, city services deteriorated with few alternatives available for residents. Garbage went uncollected, roads were made impassable by snow and potholes, and basic services like police and fire protection suffered. When local governments collapsed, new problems arose. Utilities, such as gas and electric companies, suddenly had no valid service contracts, because the cities with which they had contracted no longer existed. Their physical infrastructure gave them de facto monopolies, but the lack of contracts meant that they were free to increase their rates, and many did so dramatically. Since streets were unowned and uncontrolled, entrepreneurs began running competing water and power lines down them, sometimes in hastily constructed enclosures bolted to roads, and sometimes buried a few inches below the ground next to sidewalks. Sometimes, unauthorized crews simply dug up roads and installed utility lines.

Most neighborhoods initially dealt with the chaos of the early 2040s by creating or strengthening homeowner associations. These associations negotiated contracts with utility providers, fire control companies, and protection firms, and claimed ownership of streets. They usually required homeowners to join and pay dues, and placed restrictive covenants on their property deeds requiring the owners to comply with the rules of the association. Failure to join usually meant lack of access to utilities, services, and streets, and so was not an option for most homeowners.

Many of these homeowner associations still exist, and some have successfully maintained stable communities. The degree of regulation varies a great deal; some are rigidly controlled, with complex rules about property appearance and homeowner lifestyles, while others are more lax. Most associations are governed by elected councils, are nonprofit, and operate something like mini-governments. Increasingly, however, homeowner associations are disbanding and selling to for-profit housing companies.

In a typical conversion, a neighborhood of anywhere between 50 and 250 houses votes to sell all of its streets and land to a housing company. The company then leases individual parcels back to the homeowners for terms varying from one month to ninety-nine years. Rental payments can be fixed, variable, or tied to commercial indices. The company provides services, enforces rules, mediates disputes between tenants, helps tenants to sublease if they need to move before their lease expires, and earns profits if its rental income exceeds its expenses.

The spectacular success of housing companies in many neighborhoods, and the failures of many homeowner associations, have accelerated the trend away from homeowner associations in recent years. A similar trend has emerged for commercial properties; large commercial districts have been purchased by for-profit companies and leased space back to individual businesses. Companies with significant land holdings often join citywide organizations that promote the city to immigrants and businesses and coordinate transportation and utility services, but these organizations typically have limited influence in cities; they are nothing like municipal governments.

The growth of for-profit housing and commercial district property owners has changed the feel of large cities in Free America. Streets are meticulously clean, safe, and pleasant. Soft music plays along sidewalks, and enclosed streets are climate controlled. Moving walkways carry pedestrians past entertainment and advertising displays. A variety of innovations has made parking easier and cheaper. At the same time, smaller, older cities that began declining in the mid-twentieth century have evolved in a different direction as poor immigrants have crowded into patched-together ramshackle buildings, with factories, workshops, restaurants, shops, and apartments all on top of each other. Both kinds of cities are growing in population and wealth, and both are important parts of the Free American economy.

Exclusive Neighborhoods and Towns

Many communities, both those owned by housing companies and those controlled by homeowner associations, are exclusive in some respect. The ability to exclude residents has led to an explosion in the number of specialized neighborhoods. The united states used to prohibit discriminatory real estate sales and rentals, and allowed free public access to most streets and highways. In Free America, the sale and rental of property are limited only by private contracts.

Some communities allow free access to tourists and visitors, while others do not. Some are so closed and secretive that few on the outside have any idea of what goes on inside them. Children are born within the walls of some of these towns and grow up with no knowledge of the outside world. Protection firms have been unwilling to forcibly enter these communities unless credible evidence is shown that one of their clients is being held against his or her will. The trickiest cases have been those under family protection policies when covered children run off to join exclusive communities. There have been cases in which parents have asked protection firms to retrieve their children, and violent confrontations have erupted between community and protection firm agents. In recent years, however, exclusive communities have found that it is to their benefit to maintain good relationships with outside protection firms. For example, disgruntled former residents have attacked the drinking water supplies of exclusive communities, and in order to prosecute these attackers, the communities were obliged to work with outside protection firms.

Most exclusive communities, however, welcome new residents who fit in with their lifestyles, and one can apply to join these communities on their websites. Some exclusive communities have their own protection agencies, while others allow residents to contract with national firms. It is important to understand that if you join a community without the protection of an outside firm, you are at the mercy of the community, and no outside help should be expected if you get into trouble.

A common type of exclusive community is a religious neighborhood centered on a church. New residents are often required to sign a declaration of faith and join the church, and can be expelled for violating community or church rules. In contrast, "free love" communities screen residents for sexually transmitted diseases, prohibit marriage contracts, and give rental discounts for physically attractive residents. Some of these communities exclude children, while others are experimenting with communal child care. Other communities require proof of certain levels of wealth and education, while others require new residents to be approved by all current residents.

There are some towns and neighborhoods in Free America that are exclusively white, and others that are exclusively black. They have become popular tourist destinations for travelers around the world who are curious to see what it feels like to be in a mono-racial community, since racial integration has become mandatory in many parts of the world. The history of all-black towns in Oklahoma during the late nineteenth and early twentieth centuries has been rediscovered, and many have been established throughout Free America, particularly in the South. Some large rural areas also enforce racial exclusion through their protection agencies, primarily Native American areas in the West and European white areas in the West and Midwest. Anyone of an excluded race entering these areas is given a GPS monitoring badge at a roadside checkpoint or airport, and must surrender the badge when leaving. Entry is only permitted under certain circumstances, and anyone who enters but is not reported as leaving within a certain time is tracked down and escorted out of the area.

Most city neighborhoods, however, are not exclusive on the basis of race or nationality, and many neighborhoods in large cities are very diverse. The vibrancy of these neighborhoods is attractive for many Free Americans, who choose to live in them for their economic opportunities and freedom from community rules.

Political Cities

During the early years of Free America, attempts were made to establish new governments in several cities, but none succeeded against the majorities that refused to pay taxes or obey governmental authorities. Owners of streets refused to sell for prices that potential governments could credibly commit to pay. As a result, many who believed in government established new communities in which every resident agreed to abide by laws passed by elected representatives. Most of these new communities were very small towns, but two sizable cities experimented with new local governments, New Washington and Debsville.

New Washington attracted both private investment and money from foreign governments. A local government bureaucracy was established that purchased land, planned the city, and laid out streets. New residents purchased lots from the city government and constructed homes and businesses in accordance with the city plan. Attracting immigrants who liked the familiarity of a government-like structure, the city grew to 150,000 residents in five years. Taxes in New Washington were quite high, however, and city services were noticeably inferior to those of other cities. A privatization political party soon emerged, backed financially by national street operators, and took control of the city council. Most city streets have now been sold to private operators (although using 999-year leases) and most city services have now been privatized. At present, there is a new political party advocating the abandonment of the remnants of city government.

The founders of Debsville had a very different goal—the establishment of a socialist alternative to Free American capitalism. Leftists who were unhappy with Free America and leftists from around the world attempted to establish a city where all means of production were collectively owned. Families are assigned to houses constructed by the city, food produced on a collective farm is distributed door to door, and clothing and other goods are available for free in city-owned shops. Hoarding and resale of food and clothing is prohibited; houses and outgoing vehicles can be inspected for illegal quantities of goods. Families are issued nontransferable coupons with which they can obtain goods in shops.

Residents of Debsville work in two city-owned factories, the collective farm, and other public facilities, such as schools and community centers. Jobs are assigned by the city after taking account of resident's preferred ordering of jobs and qualifications. There is no pay; work is required, and the distribution of consumer goods is unaffected by occupation or work. Goods produced in the factories are sold by a city agency and the proceeds are used to buy supplies needed in the city.

Funded initially by several wealthy individuals and a few foreign governments, Debsville's population grew for a few years until it peaked at fifty thousand residents, but then shrank as residents became dissatisfied with their low standard of living. The discovery of embezzlement of funds by city officials further shook the confidence of residents, and the population of Debsville is now officially twenty thousand, but many people believe that the actual figure is lower.

Initially, anyone refusing to work as required was expelled from the community, but as the population dropped, this policy appears to have changed. It is believed that the city now sells shirkers to incarceration companies. This is possible, since residents agree not to contract with outside protection firms, so it would be difficult for them to resist being sold.

Housing Quality

A much greater variety of housing quality is available now than when local governments regulated construction. Immigrants now crowd into tenements in inner cities and near suburban factories. While rents are very cheap in these rough housing projects, newly built apartments are no longer required to have anti-fire sprinkler systems, or to have individual kitchens and bathrooms. Japanese-style capsule living is becoming more popular in some cities, where individuals can rent a box that is just big enough to sleep in, stacked on top of other sleeping boxes. These projects contain shared bathroom and eating facilities. It is possible in most cities to earn enough in two hours of unskilled work to rent decent accommodations with meals for a night.

The cost of luxury housing has also plummeted in recent years. Huge new suburban developments now surround most cities and towns. You should investigate the quality of the infrastructure of these developments before buying, however. Sewage, water, electrical, and communication connections in some new developments proved to be of very low quality and failed soon after all of the houses in the developments were sold. Guarantees were often backed only by corporations that had been drained of assets by the time problems were noticed. Houses are often built to less exacting specifications than used to be the case when government officials inspected and required permits for every renovation and construction project. The lack of quality standards helps to make new houses much cheaper, and many buyers are not interested in features that used to be required, such as wide staircases and hallways, energy efficiency systems, and fire sprinklers. Because corners can be cut in ways that were once not allowed, many people can afford much larger houses than before.

Company Towns

While most cities and towns contain competing neighborhoods, owned either through homeowner and business associations or for-profit housing and business district operators, there are some that are entirely owned by a single company. Many of these cities have been constructed from scratch on previously unoccupied land. Often referred to as "company towns," they are nothing like the coal mining towns of the nineteenth century that the term evokes. Even during that period, historians now report, company towns offered more choice and a far better standard of living than many believe.

The primary difference between company and other towns and cities relates to planning. Company towns are planned in meticulous detail. The visions of planners differ substantially from project to project, but in all of them, every aspect of the city fits in with an overall plan. Some of these cities are built around a specific industry, while others have diverse economies. Some screen residents, but most are competing with other cities to gain population, and so will accept residents with clear backgrounds and some job skills. Most company towns offer long-term leases for houses and apartments upon acceptance of a job.

Practical Advice

When you rent or purchase real estate, the lease or deed should be registered immediately with your protection firm. It is important to read the rules attached to a lease or the covenants attached to a deed, for they will tell you about your obligations to your new community—everything from the rules about shoveling snow and painting your house to required participation in neighborhood watch programs and approved protection firms.

Housing inspectors are available in every city, and it is a good idea to find a reputable one to investigate a house or apartment that you are considering buying or renting. Your protection firm should also review the property to make sure that the seller or landlord legitimately owns it. Decent, low-cost housing is available everywhere, but renters and buyers must be cautious.

5

Protecting Yourself

In your home country, you probably relied on government police for protection against crime. In Free America, however, there are no government police, so you are responsible for your own protection. Inside the immigrant complex, your protection is guaranteed by the firm that owns it. Before you leave the complex, however, it is very important that you obtain a contract with a protection firm. There are many firms from which to choose. General Security is the largest one, and it offers long-term contracts to new immigrants. Other companies offer contracts at a lower cost, but you may find that they are less aggressive in protecting your welfare in certain cases.

Protection Contracts

A protection contract obligates you to follow the rules of the protection firm, and obligates the firm to protect you against crimes committed by others. In recent years, the insurance and protection industries have merged, and most large protection firms will immediately pay compensation to the victim of a crime, and will then attempt to recover their costs from the perpetrator's protection firm, which will, in turn, recover their costs from the perpetrator. In many cases, a firm will punish an offender beyond what is required for simple restitution.

The protection firm's liability when a crime is committed is limited to the amount that it can extract from the offender. This limitation is necessary, because otherwise, a protection firm would have an incentive to hide crimes committed by its customers. If, for example, a protection firm learned that one of its customers had kidnapped several people and was holding them in his basement, the protection firm might worry that disclosing the crime would require it to compensate all of the victims, and the cost of compensation would be greater than anything it could ever obtain from the customer. Since its liability is limited, the protection firm knows that it will recover any cost it incurs by reporting the crime, plus fees from which it will earn some profit. As long as it is perceived to be fair in its treatment of the offender, it will not alienate its other customers by prosecuting the offender, and it will earn the firm credit with other protection firms, making future cooperation that much easier.

Criminal procedure in Free America depends on the level of protection that has been purchased. While the procedures are based on those followed by the old united states government, the protection offered to those accused of crimes has been categorized into four levels: A, B, C, and D. Level A protection imposes a high burden of proof for the determination of guilt and has high standards regarding the evidence that can be admitted. The accused can opt for a jury trial, and private property will only be searched if there is probable cause to suspect a crime. Levels B and C weaken these protections in various ways, and level D essentially allows a protection firm to determine guilt or innocence through an informal review of evidence, and to enter the customer's home unannounced to search for evidence of crimes.

Level A protection is quite expensive, particularly for anyone with a criminal record, or with characteristics that would lead a protection firm to believe that future criminal activity is likely. Most people opt for level B protection, which does not allow jury trials, limits appeals, and allows a wider range of evidence than level A protection. The costs of criminal investigations are much lower under level B protection than under level A protection, so level B protection contracts are much cheaper. Most people believe that constant personal GPS monitoring and video surveillance reduce the risk of false accusation of a crime, so the savings are worth the loss of protection.

If a client has an extensive criminal record, protection firms believe that the odds are high that they will have to investigate and prosecute crimes; so they are only willing to provide greater than level D protection if protection contract premiums are very high.

It is important to note that paying for an expensive level A protection contract does not in any way guarantee a finding of innocence in case of a criminal accusation. Final determination of guilt is done by an impartial arbitration firm that will go to great lengths to protect its reputation of impartiality.

A series of scandals involving protection firms that dropped clients as soon as they needed protection led to the development of one-way constant-horizon contracts. In this arrangement, clients are able to cancel a protection contract without notice, but protection firms agree to a certain term (typically five years) that, at the discretion of the firm, extends another five years every year. With this contract, a firm canceling a contract must give at least four years' notice to the client, allowing him time to make other arrangements. Certain events, such as the completion of a term of incarceration for a serious crime, also enable a protection firm to cancel a contract.

Cooperation between Protection Firms

All protection firms have rules against common crimes such as theft, assault, and murder. A common core of crimes has been defined by the Association of Free America Protection Firms (AFAPF). Members of AFAPF are estimated to have contracts with 92 percent of all residents of Free America, but such estimates are difficult to verify. Firms belonging to AFAPF all have established procedures for cooperating with each other and arbitrating disputes. The AFAPF also rates the performance of its members using independent auditors, and those falling below certain standards can lose their membership. All protection contracts with firms in the AFAPF contain clauses that permit the contract to be broken by the customer if the firm loses membership in AFAPF. Customers in disputes with their protection firm may also appeal to a review committee of the AFAPF council, which has the contractual power to release customers from their protection contracts.

All protection firms have agreements with other protection firms that govern how they will interact if one of their clients is accused of a crime against the clients of the other firm. Rules of protection agencies can differ substantially. For example, Acme Security, based in Reno, does not recognize blackmail as a crime, while General Security, based in Greenwich, does. Clients of Acme Security cannot obtain restitution or punish anyone who, for example, obtains embarrassing photographs and demands money to keep them off of the Internet. But because General Security does protect its clients against blackmail, clients of Acme Security can still be prosecuted if they blackmail a client of General Security.

Standards for fraud in financial transactions differ among firms. If you are involved in business transactions, you or your attorney must be familiar with the protections offered by the protection firm of the person you are dealing with. The legal costs of doing business with clients of firms such as Acme are quite low, since they will very seldom prosecute cases of fraud, but, of course, the risk to their clients of being defrauded is greater. If you are involved in a financial transaction with a client of General Security, however, you must make sure that everything about the transaction is in accordance with its rules, for if you break them, your protection firm will be unable to prevent your punishment.

In the early days of Free America, there was worry about protection firms with very restrictive laws; for example, what if a firm offered to protect clients against insults? Anyone with such a contract might walk down the street hurling insults at residents of an area dominated by a protection agency that did not provide the same protection. When insulted in return, they could call on their own protection firms to arrest the offender and extract restitution. To quiet these fears, protection firms began to offer protection against entrapment, so that the person doing the insulting with the intent of prosecuting a return insult would also be guilty of an offense. In practice, protection firms do not offer protection against things like simple insults, because the costs of enforcing it and the difficulties it presents for cooperation with other protection firms are higher than what clients are willing to pay.

The basic rule in Free America is as follows: do not do anything to other people that their protection firm protects them against. Most protection firms have adopted very similar rules in most situations. Rules that are more restrictive than normal are widely publicized, and these rules have caused many people to avoid the conduct in question if there is any doubt about which protection agency with which a person has a contract.

Years ago, wearing a badge indicating which protection agency a person was affiliated with was a popular practice, but as the rules and procedures became increasingly standardized, the popularity of these badges declined. A few protection firms with unusual contracts require their clients to wear badges when they are traveling in certain areas.

How the System Works

Suppose you have a protection contract with General Security and you steal a car from a person who has a contract with another firm such as Protection Unlimited. Protection Unlimited will immediately compensate the owner for the value of the car and conduct an investigation to determine the identity of the thief. When they learn that it was you who stole the car, they will notify your protection firm, General Security, and because the two firms have agreed to cooperate with each other, General Security will require you to report to one of their offices. If you do not appear, their security agents will find you and bring you in. A hearing will be held at which Protection Unlimited will present its evidence against you. Your security firm will defend you based on the information you provide to them. General Security will also offer you the option of hiring an advocate to help you present your case. Some protection firms require that advocates be approved in advance by the firm, while others allow you to hire any advocate of your choice.

If after the hearing, your protection firm is not convinced of your guilt, the two protection firms will appeal to an arbitration firm that they have previously agreed to use. If your protection firm agrees with Protection Unlimited that you are guilty of theft, they will pay Protection Unlimited the value of the car, plus the cost of the investigation and hearings. If you have paid extra for an appeal clause in your contract, you may appeal this decision to a previously agreed upon arbitration firm. If not, or if you lose your appeal, General Security will ask you to compensate them for twice their costs (note that the multiple may vary according to your contract and the agreements between the protection firms). If you pay, the amount in excess of simple restitution will be divided between the victim and the two protection firms.

If you cannot or will not pay this amount, then General Security will place you in an incarceration facility, perhaps one owned by General Security, Protection Unlimited, or a third party. Some protection contracts narrow the choice of incarceration facility, but others leave the choice up to the protection firms. For some crimes, you might be required to spend time in an incarceration facility in addition to paying restitution and fines. A third-party incarceration firm will usually pay a lump sum amount to your protection firm, and this amount would depend on the length of time specified by your protection contract for the crime of car theft, and the incarceration firm's estimate of your productivity. At the incarceration facility, you will work, and the incarceration firm will attempt to earn back the amount they paid to your protection firm with the product of your efforts. Your protection firm will also monitor your condition in the incarceration facility.

Upon your release, your protection firm may decline future coverage, and you will be forced to find a firm that specializes in clients with a criminal record. These firms are costlier than other protection firms, often do not provide appeal services, and may require you to use only advocates employed by the protection firm.

Guards and Patrols

Protection firms also provide security guards that patrol neighborhoods and guard businesses. Neighborhoods of individual homeowners often require all residents to contract with a single protection firm, because all residents benefit from these patrols. These requirements are enforced through deed covenants on real estate; hence, purchasing a particular house may require you to contract with a particular protection firm. Neighborhoods owned by housing companies renting property to residents offer basic security as part of the lease, but renters will also need an additional protection contract. It is, of course, possible to have contracts with several protection firms. One contract might protect your home, another might protect your business, and another might protect you while traveling. Many protection firms also offer home and automobile insurance and free fire protection services along with the insurance.

Charitable Protection

Charitable protection firms do exist, and larger protection firms take on some cases on a pro bono basis. The greatest demand for these services is among those with no protection contract, either because of failure to pay premiums, or the past commission of crimes that prevents other protection firms from offering coverage.

Individuals who sign waivers indicating that they have no protection contract are offered accommodation and employment by some landlords and employers. If disputes arise, however, there is no way for a person without a protection contract to prevent the seizure of assets, or even imprisonment, unless a charitable protection firm intervenes. In one recent case, a homeless day laborer was accused of rape. The accuser's protection firm arrested the laborer and was about to sell him to an incarceration firm when he managed to steal a phone from a guard and call Stand By Me, a charitable protection firm. Stand By Me, which had agreements with the accuser's protection firm, requested a hearing, at which it was discovered that the laborer was innocent. Some protection firms in this situation automatically allow accused people with no protection agency to contact a charitable protection agency, but others prefer to avoid possible complications and publicity and simply sell them to incarceration firms.

There is some debate among Free Americans about the desirability of charitable protection firms. Some protection firms argue that the existence of such firms convinces many people to go without protection contracts, reasoning that they can call a charitable firm if the need arises. Others point out that charitable firms have nowhere near the capability of defending every person in Free America without a protection contract, so there is plenty of incentive for people to pay for protection.

It is also possible to pay for the protection of other individuals. An imprisoned man with no protection contract recently got word to his sister, who paid her protection firm to investigate her brother's case. Because the sister was willing to pay all costs, the protection agency of the accuser in the case agreed to an investigation and hearing that eventually cleared her brother. Incarceration firms depend on protection firms for business, so most of them are responsive to requests for investigations and hearings on prisoners if new evidence arises. Some allow prisoners limited communication with the outside world, but others, wary of these communications being used to coordinate escapes, allow no communication or visits. Of course, high-quality protection contracts contain provisions that prevent incarceration in these types of facilities.

Reducing Protection Contract Costs

Premiums on protection contracts vary widely between companies, and even between clients of the same protection firm. Taking certain steps can save a significant amount of money, and may also enhance your security.

The best way to obtain first-class protection at a minimal cost is to convince a protection firm that you will not commit crimes that they will have to pay for. Crimes committed by others are usually paid for by the perpetrator's protection firm, but crimes that you commit are costly to your protection firm, both monetarily and in damage to the firm's reputation. The more monitoring you submit to, the more your protection firm will be convinced that you have no intention of committing crimes, and the lower your rates will be.

Criminals see the situation differently; they believe that less monitoring reduces their chances of being caught, and they also think it reduces the chances of a loss for the protection firm. Protection firms, however, have learned that often, clients who refuse any monitoring are eventually caught in other ways, and turn out to be very expensive clients. Monitoring can take the form of GPS tracking, hidden cameras and microphones installed in eyeglasses or jewelry, and cameras in cars.

A record of criminal activity often eliminates the possibility of an individual receiving protection from top firms and significantly raises the cost of a contract with a firm specializing in clients with criminal records. If you are a member of an age group, ethnic group, or racial group with a statistically high crime rate, your rates may be higher than others; nevertheless, the maintenance of a clean record and acceptance of some level of surveillance are far more important factors in setting premiums.

Why Don't Protection Firms Fight Each Other?

People in government controlled countries often express amazement that Free America hasn't descended into chaos and violence. They wonder how protection firms manage to settle disputes without going to war with each other. Free Americans believe that our system of social organization is an advance, just as representative democracy was an advance over absolute monarchies. When representative democracy was first proposed, it would have seemed just as mysterious to monarchists as Free America does to believers in government. Why wouldn't the loser of an election simply assassinate the winner? Why wouldn't the winner of an election refuse to hold more elections?

The answer is that the mores of society are different in Free America than in other countries, just as the mores of successful representative democracies were different than those of monarchies. Protection firms have become accustomed to settling disputes through negotiation and arbitration rather than by force, and their customers and competitors would not allow them to behave differently. Any protection firm attempting to settle a dispute by force would quickly lose the support of its suppliers, partners, and customers.

Like other industries, the protection business is competitive, and no single firm dominates the industry. No firm is large enough to impose its will on the entire system. It appears that diseconomies of scale have become important at fairly small-sized firms, so if any protection firm grows too large, smaller, more nimble firms will begin to take business away from it. Without very large firms, no single firm ever sees an advantage in fighting against the system as a whole.

It is possible, of course, that some crisis may cause this system to break down, just as the American system of federalism broke down during the Civil War of the 1860s. Free Americans are becoming increasingly confident, however, that our system is more stable than governmental and political systems.

Who Keeps Protection Firms Accountable?

This is a question often asked by people unfamiliar with the Free American system. Being used to the idea of government as an ultimate arbiter and enforcer of contracts has led them to believe that such an entity is necessary for society to function properly. Free Americans ask in return, "What keeps governments accountable?" After all, elections can be rigged, and constitutional guarantees can be ignored by people in power. No society can offer ironclad guarantees of anything—all human institutions require some amount of trust in order to operate.

In Free America, the primary force that keeps protection firms accountable is competition. A protection firm that does not live up to its promises quickly earns a bad reputation and loses business. The largest and most profitable protection firms are those who have developed good reputations by living up to their contracts. After years of experience with protection firms, and after hearing of the experiences of others, people come to trust their protection firms. This trust represents a significant capital asset to protection firms, and they are careful to guard it.

Will a Protection Firm Eventually Become the Government?

Dozens of large protection firms operate in every Free American city. Every attempt by protection firms to form monopolistic cartels has broken down as dissatisfied customers have switched companies. Some firms have attempted to require customers to sign long-duration contracts, but they have proven to be unenforceable, because customers' new protection firms resist enforcement actions of previous protection firms.

Many protection firms operate nationally, but national market shares of these companies are much smaller than local market shares of large firms in individual cities. No firm seems remotely able to dominate a single large city, let alone the entire country.

There are small towns in which a single protection firm operates. Some of these towns are closed to outsiders, so it is possible that the protection firms operate as governments, even tyrannical governments, in these areas. More commonly, however, in towns with single protection firms, residents obtain "monitor" contracts with other firms that are acknowledged by the primary protection firm. These monitor contracts allow other protection firms to monitor the town and to intervene in the event that the primary protection firm violates its contract. In extreme cases, the monitoring firm can evacuate residents of towns with an unsatisfactory protection firm.

It is impossible to predict the future, but most Free Americans believe that it would be impossible for a protection firm or group of protection firms to take over Free America and establish a government.

Example Cases

The protection business causes more confusion than any other issue for new immigrants, probably because of wild rumors that are common around the world in government-controlled countries. It is important to remember, however, that the streets in most Free American cities are among the safest in the world. While our system of justice is innovative and different from any other in the world, it actually works very well. To give you a better idea of how justice is done in Free America, below are a few examples of cases that have arisen in recent years.

Indecent Exposure

On a street in Chicago, Mr. A indecently exposed himself to Ms. B on a sidewalk owned by ABC Properties. Ms. B immediately called her protection firm, All Safe, which sent an armed security guard to join an ABC security agent to find and arrest Mr. A. When he was arrested, Mr. A denied exposing himself and called his protection firm, Safety First, to complain of an unlawful arrest. All three firms—Safety First, All Safe, and ABC—reviewed video surveillance footage from a street camera and concluded that Mr. A had indeed exposed himself. All Safe then paid Ms. B the amount specified in her contract as damages for indecent exposure. Mr. A's contract with Safety First did not include indecent exposure among the prohibited activities, but the rules posted by ABC Properties on the Internet did prohibit such conduct; so, Safety First compensated All Safe and ABC Properties for their costs, plus damages to ABC Properties for loss of business and reputation. Furthermore, Safety First recovered its payment from Mr. A's bank, because Mr. A's agreement with the bank allowed his protection firm to debit funds in the event of a conviction of a crime.

Ms. B's protection contract also called for a term of imprisonment for anyone guilty of this crime against her in All Safe's incarceration facility. Therefore, Safety First released Mr. A into the custody of All Safe for incarceration. Safety First monitored Mr. A's incarceration, making sure that conditions were adequate, communications were established, and that he was released as scheduled. Ms. B also had the option of monitoring Mr. A's incarceration.

On his release, Safety First dropped Mr. A's contract, and he was forced to sign a much more expensive contract with less protection with Budget Protection. After ten years with no offenses entered into any of the criminal databases, Mr. A reapplied to Safety First and was able to sign a new contract.

Animal Cruelty

Mr. C purchased a home in the Woods neighborhood of Anytown. The deed covenant associated with his property prohibits acts of animal cruelty. Mr. C beat and starved his dog, and his neighbors eventually noticed. The neighborhood association's protection firm contacted Mr. C's protection firm and presented evidence that he had violated the deed covenant. Mr. C's protection firm was convinced of the violation, so it informed Mr. C that it would not protect him against an eviction and forced the sale of his property. Mr. C refused to leave his house, so the neighborhood association's protection firm sent security guards to eject him forcibly. The neighborhood association then registered its ownership of Mr. C's house after making a payment to Mr. C in accordance with the deed covenant. Since Mr. C's protection firm did not object to the forced sale, the property registration company accepted the sale and recorded it over Mr. C's objections.

In another animal rights case, a ranch in rural Nebraska raised hogs in a confinement facility. An animal rights group in Chicago objected, broke into the property, and freed several hogs. Before taking this action, the animal rights group established a protection firm that they said represented the hogs on the ranch. The rancher's protection firm obtained permission from the landlord who owned the apartment complex in which the offenders lived to arrest them in their apartments. Because the rancher's and landlord's protection firms had no relationship with the animal rights group's new protection firm, it ignored their objections to the arrest. The members of the animal rights groups quickly made restitution for the freed hogs.

Pedophilia

Although most protection firms prohibit sex between children and adults, until 2039, ABC protection firm had no such provision. Mr. D, a pedophile, signed a protection contract with ABC. He bought an isolated piece of land with no deed restrictions on his behavior, purchased children in other countries, and brought them back to his land. He invited pedophiles from across the country to come to his land to take advantage of the children. Neighbors suspected what was happening and eventually trespassed on his land to gather evidence. Mr. D contacted his protection agency to prosecute his neighbors for trespass. The neighbors publicized what was happening, and there was a national outcry. Other protection firms announced that they would no longer cooperate with ABC, and the neighbors' protection firm announced that it would defend its clients against arrest for trespass. Without cooperation from other protection firms, clients of ABC began to worry that if crimes were committed against them, ABC would not be able to obtain restitution or punish the offenders, so many cancelled their contracts and switched to other firms. Seeing significant loss of business, ABC announced that it would continue to protect Mr. D against arrest and seizure of his property, but would not protect him from a seizure of the children on his property. Mr. D's neighbors entered the property, seized the children and brought them to a charitable orphanage. ABC then added pedophilia as a prohibited activity.

Killing in Self-Defense

Mr. E and Mr. F argued and fought, and Mr. F was killed. Mr. F's protection firm contacted Mr. E's protection firm, which allowed Mr. F's protection firm to arrest Mr. E. Mr. E claimed that he had acted in self-defense, and his protection firm eventually agreed, but Mr. F's protection firm did not. In accordance with his contract, Mr. E was moved to a luxury incarceration facility while the appeal was pending. Several luxury incarceration facilities have been constructed recently to solve the problem of defendants whose guilt has not been agreed upon but who might pose a threat to others. An arbitration firm agreed to by both protection firms heard the case and determined that Mr. E had acted in self-defense, and he was released. Details of the case were added to public databases, and the costs of the investigation, hearing, and incarceration were deducted from Mr. F's estate, which contained money obtained from the sale of several of his organs.

Defamation

Ms. G published an article falsely claiming that Mr. H had committed terrible crimes. The protection contracts of both of them covered defamation causing significant damages, and Mr. H demonstrated to his protection firm that the defamation had caused a loss of business. Ms. G's protection firm negotiated a settlement amount, withdrew enough money to cover the damages from Ms. G's bank account, and ordered Ms. G to remove the article from the Internet or lose coverage. Ms. G complied, although the article had been reproduced by several other websites. At Ms. G's expense, the owners of these websites were informed of the result of Mr. H's complaint, and the articles were removed.

A trickier case of defamation involved a website that attempted to list every person in Free America and allowed anonymous contributors to leave comments about anyone. Millions of people complained publicly on the site about their neighbors, relatives, bosses, co-workers, romantic rivals, business clients, etc. The website's owner, a very wealthy company, had a protection contract that prohibited defamation, but the company claimed that it had not defamed anyone any more than the owner of a wall on which others had written graffiti.

A prominent psychologist who had attracted hundreds of very negative comments charged the website owner with defamation. His protection firm and that of the website owner disagreed, and the arbitration firm agreed upon by the two firms ruled that the psychologist had been defamed and was owed significant damages. Seeing an opportunity for profit, protection agencies encouraged their clients who had been insulted on the website to bring charges as well.

Facing bankruptcy, the website owner's protection firm launched a secret investigation into the arbitrator that had ruled against them and found that he had been bribed by attorneys hoping to use his ruling to profit from future litigation. The website owner's protection firm charged the arbitrator with violating the terms of the arbitration contract. The arbitrator's protection agency, also hoping to profit from litigation, did not agree to the charges, and the case went to another arbitrator. This arbitrator ruled against the first arbitrator and was able to reverse the original decision because of an anticorruption clause in the original contract.

This case led to a significant increase in the professionalization of the arbitration industry. Instead of single individuals who could be tempted, particularly near retirement, to take a bribe to influence a decision, protection firms increasingly used only large arbitration companies, which depended on reputation for business, and whose stock prices depended on maintaining their reputations into the distant future.

6

Punishment of Crimes

For most nonviolent crimes, the only punishment in Free America is full restitution plus an additional monetary payment, with total payment usually equal to twice the original damages. The amount of payment is determined by the protection firms of the criminal and the victim. In most cases, these payments have been standardized, but they are subject to negotiation between protection firms. Required payments for repeat offenses escalate quickly.

For violent crimes, most protection contracts require that upon conviction, an offender be turned over to an incarceration firm. The offender's protection firm will, in some cases, monitor conditions in prison, but is usually not required to continue protection after a sentence has been served.

Prisons

Prison inmates perform a variety of work and usually live in spartan conditions. Depending on the existence and terms of an inmate's protection contract, a prisoner who refuses to work or who causes trouble in prison can be executed. The organs of executed prisoners are usually sold to medical facilities for transplantation.

Cooperative, productive prisoners, however, are adequately fed, clothed, and housed. Rewards for good work are often offered, although punishments for poor productivity are also given. Workdays are typically twelve hours, six days per week. The work usually involves manufacturing or agriculture, but prisoners with special skills are often assigned other work. In some cases, work is performed outside of the prison itself, and the prisoners are leased to other businesses. In these cases, electronic monitoring is used to prevent escape.

The treatment of prisoners is also determined by the terms of their protection contracts. When an incarceration facility pays a protection firm for an inmate, it agrees to abide by the firm's conditions as stipulated in the protection contract. Work hours and living conditions are often specified in great detail. For prisoners with less expensive protection contracts, however, the incarceration facility is free to offer whatever conditions it believes will maximize inmate productivity.

Capital Punishment

Capital punishment is given for some crimes, again, depending on the terms of protection contracts. For example, some protection contracts promise capital punishment for anyone found guilty of murdering one of the protection firm's clients. No protection firm will be able to prevent the execution of a client found guilty of murdering someone with this kind of contract. Protection firm marketing studies have shown that clients with contracts promising capital punishment are less likely to be murdered than clients with more lenient contracts, and this has increased demand for capital punishment contracts. While a murdered client obviously cannot pursue the prosecution of a murderer, the client's protection firm does pursue these cases to prove to its remaining clients that it takes their protection seriously.

Debt

Failure to pay debts is treated as a breach of contract, and debt contracts spell out the consequences of failure to pay. Some debt contracts specify very limited recourse; for example, certain property might be seized, but nothing else. Other contracts allow property seizure and garnishment of wages. Others allow a creditor to sell a borrower to an incarceration facility for whatever term is required to pay the debt. In extreme cases, debt contracts have been written that allow creditors to sell borrowers to medical facilities for their organs, but very few reputable medical facilities admit to engaging in these kinds of transactions. It is unknown whether this practice continues, but if it does, it probably involves very few borrowers. It is, however, very important to read debt contracts carefully and to have your protection firm review them.

"Slavery" Controversy

Many prisoners are currently serving very long or even life sentences in incarceration facilities. Skilled prisoners who are not considered violent are commonly leased out to businesses to perform services. The most common prisoners considered for leased work are those who have been imprisoned for failure to pay debts. This practice has been likened to slavery, since the workers are unable to change jobs as they wish, and do not control their own earnings. Leased workers are usually given some incentive pay, however, because employers have discovered that workers are more productive if they are rewarded for their efforts. Incentive pay tends to be far lower than pay for comparable work by non-leased employees, and it is accompanied by punishments, sometimes physical, for poor work performance.

In some cases, individuals who need money to pay a debt, pay for a medical procedure for themselves or a relative, or who simply desire a way to raise capital for a future project will sell themselves to an incarceration firm for some length of time. The individuals who choose this option are those who are unable to sell their future income on public stock markets due to a poor work history. Some sell a percentage of their earnings and retain some control of the type of work they will perform, but prices for these contracts tend to be lower than those contracts where an incarceration firm retains complete control.

In many offices, employees and customers are unaware of the leased status of their co-workers. Some leased workers are allowed to live in their own housing away from the incarceration site, albeit with electronic monitoring. In Free America, leased worker status has gradually come to be accepted, and leased workers have even formed promotional associations to improve their image in society.

Foreign antislavery activists have made a cause célèbre of freeing leased workers in Free America. In many instances, activists have entered Free America, stolen leased workers, and taken them abroad. Some leased workers have welcomed their capture, often joining the lucrative European lecture circuit denouncing the evils of Free America. In several incidences, however, activists have been embarrassed by leased workers who wished to stay in Free America, and have fought and in some cases killed activists attempting to "rescue" them.

The Incarceration Business

Incarceration firms keep the product of the work performed by inmates. They pay protection firms for inmates, who use the money to pay restitution to victims, and to pay their own costs. In order to profit, incarceration firms must obtain more from an inmate's work than they pay to protection firms. Furthermore, they are restrained in their exploitation of inmates by these protection firms, which monitor the conditions of the incarceration facility.

The incarceration business was immensely profitable for several years. During the 2030s and 2040s, old government prisons were often purchased for very little money, and they contained ready-made workforces. Lacking any kind of protection contract, most of these prisoners were subject to harsh, inexpensive working environments. The incarceration industry established vast manufacturing and agricultural operations that had very low labor costs. The productivity of the inmates, low at first, gradually improved, until it was estimated in 2050 that 40 percent of Free America's manufacturing output came from incarceration firms.

The number of new inmates regularly entering incarceration facilities, however, has fallen dramatically in recent years. Constant monitoring of streets, protection premium discounts for personal location recording, and harsh punishments have almost eliminated certain kinds of crime. As the current prison population ages, is purchased by non-incarceration firms, and is offered freedom as a productivity incentive, incarceration facilities will be forced to close. Stock prices of incarceration firms have plummeted over the past few years, and many predict that independent incarceration firms may soon cease to exist, with the business taken over by the in-house incarceration operations of protection firms.

7
Money

The hyperinflation of the late 2030s caused the banking system to fail in 2040, and dollars became worthless. Individuals and businesses with bank accounts lost everything they had deposited. Only non-monetary assets like real estate, equipment, and commodities retained their value. Corporate stock retained value if the underlying companies had non-monetary assets, and if companies paid dividends in gold certificates, but bonds that promised to pay in dollars lost all of their value. Similarly, pension obligations, mortgages, and other contracts promising dollar payments became valueless. On the other hand, those with dollar-denominated debts gained, because their debts were no longer worth anything. You will still find many restaurants and bars throughout Free America with wallpaper made of old dollar currency.

Protection firms have all honored past government records indicating ownership of non-monetary assets. For example, a house with a deed recorded under a government system would be recognized as private property and protected against theft or damage. Title insurance companies in many areas have taken over the role of maintaining a central database of property ownership records. Simple possession of other assets is usually enough to establish ownership.

Without a functioning monetary system in 2040, the united states entered a terrible economic depression. The weakness of the federal government, however, quickly convinced entrepreneurs that there were no legal barriers to issuing their own currencies designed for ordinary transactions.

The infamous firm Old Gold was the first to issue gold certificates intended for use as currency. The firm began as a gold storage company for the many individuals and businesses that had purchased gold from the federal government during the auctions of the 2020s and 2030s, charging storage fees and guaranteeing security. In

2041, responding to a desperate need for currency, Old Gold began issuing gold certificates in a variety of denominations, produced by European countries. They contained numerous anti-counterfeiting features and could be redeemed for a certain amount of gold on presentation at an Old Gold office. These certificates quickly became popular for ordinary transactions such as paying employees and buying retail items.

In the freewheeling early 2040s, there were few restraints on financial activity. Most of the larger businesses operated without outside protection contracts, employing their own security personnel as needed. Unfortunately, the lack of independent oversight of financial firms led to many abuses. The most prominent example was Old Gold, which secretly printed large amounts of gold certificates for which it held no gold. As long as redemption requests stayed low, this strategy was sustainable and enormously profitable. By confusing auditors about which gold it owned and which was being stored for others, Old Gold maintained confidence in the value of its certificates.

Knowing, however, that the truth of the nature of its business would eventually be revealed, Old Gold executives began cashing out in 2043. Through a variety of front companies, they converted certificates worth millions of ounces of gold into foreign currency that they deposited abroad. Suspicions about Old Gold appeared on a popular news website in early 2044, and a run quickly developed. Old Gold's stocks of gold were depleted two days after the run began, even though Old Gold fraudulently distributed a great deal of gold that it had merely been storing for others. Within hours of Old Gold's suspension of conversion to gold, its certificates became worthless. Dozens of Old Gold executives and investors fled to countries around the world where they are still protected from the wrath of American depositors. Others were rounded up by mobs of people and lynched in New York City's Battery Park. Mistrust quickly spread to other certificate-issuing firms, and runs uncovered other firms engaged in the same activity, although on a far smaller scale than Old Gold.

Honest certificate-issuing companies also experienced runs in 2044, but when it became clear that they were able to fully pay off all certificate holders in gold, the market value of their remaining certificates quickly rose. To bolster their credibility, these firms sought contracts with large, established protection firms, which demanded strict oversight of their activities.

The largest issuer of currency today, Money Honey, pioneered many innovative ideas. It began the practice of accepting gold deposits, issuing certificates, and then leasing out the gold to third parties wanting to use it. A large percentage of the gold jewelry worn and kept in homes throughout Free America, for example, is actually owned by Money Honey. Money Honey collects lease payments from jewelry users, but maintains the right to call them in on short notice if it is needed to redeem gold certificates. Jewelry with sentimental value that users do not want subject to a call is usually owned outright, but such ownership has become rather expensive.

Income from lease payments allows Money Honey to pay interest on gold certificates. Embedded within each certificate is a microprocessor that computes the current value of the certificate, including accrued interest, which is displayed on the currency using electronic ink. Recent issues are able to adjust values for changing interest rates, which are read wirelessly from the Internet by the currency microprocessor.

To understand how Money Honey currency works, consider the relationship between a one-gram note in your pocket and a gold necklace worn by a woman sitting next to you at the theater. A gold owner initially deposited a gram of gold with Money Honey and received a one-gram certificate. The gold was leased to a jewelry manufacturing company that manufactured the necklace and subleased it to the woman sitting next to you, who enjoys her necklace in return for small payments continuously debited from one of her financial accounts. Money Honey receives the lease payments, and the certificate it issues continually increases in value, although by less than the lease payments, allowing a profit for Money Honey. The certificate in your pocket displays its current value and is readable by vending machines. The change you receive from a purchase will depend on the current value of the certificate. If you decide that you want gold instead of currency, you can redeem the certificate with Money Honey, and if its stock of gold is insufficient to provide you with your gram of gold, it can cancel the lease with the necklace manufacturer, which will then require the woman wearing the necklace to return it. The gold you receive from Money Honey might be the necklace of the woman sitting next to you, or it might be melted down and forged into a bar of standardized weight.

Although most hand-to-hand currency is still gold-backed, more and more money is now backed by other liquid assets, such as cars, food commodities, equipment, and even leased workers. Exchange rates are easily available on the Internet, and are dynamically programmed into vending machines and retail point-of-sale equipment. Different currencies pay different rates of interest, which is reflected in the exchange rates.

Certificates can also be deposited into banks. Banks have a variety of account options for you to consider. Some accounts guarantee payment on demand and promise to hold the equivalent in cash of the certificates you deposit in their vaults. These accounts usually require payment of a continuous maintenance fee. Other accounts give the bank the right to delay repayment if they do not have sufficient cash on hand, since they lend out a portion of their cash to interest-paying borrowers. Others promise only to redeem notes for a certain fraction of the current market value of the bank's assets. Under this arrangement, there is less incentive to run to the bank to redeem notes in response to bad news, since the value that can be obtained from the bank adjusts instantly to news, reducing the incentive to be first in line. Accounts like these generally do not require maintenance fees and often pay interest.

In order to attract depositors, banks carefully disclose the percentage of your deposit that will be kept in the bank's vaults, the percentage that is lent out, and the kinds of investments the bank makes.

Another innovation of the Free American financial system is continual flow payment. Instead of making, for example, monthly payments to an electric utility company, your payments are made instantly as you use electricity. The utility company monitors your electricity usage and deducts payments from your bank account continuously as you use the electricity. Similarly, employers pay employees continuously as they work. When an electronic monitor detects the arrival of an employee, pay begins to flow from the employer bank account into the employee bank account. Regular payments such as mortgages are continuously deducted from your bank account. Money can also be continuously deposited into an investment account to earn higher returns. At any moment, you can obtain a calculation of your current account balance, netting all of the flows into and out of your account. Lump sum payments are also possible, of course, and electronic transfers can be made very cheaply using a variety of competing clearinghouses.

If you wish to borrow money, there are a variety of financial services firms from which to choose. Interest rates on loans depend on your personal characteristics, credit history, and the collateral that you offer. Moreover, some lenders vary their rates according to the age, sex, race, or national origin of the borrower. Some will not lend to people who have contracts with certain protection firms, and others will vary interest rates depending on your protection firm. The strongest collateral you can offer is a promise to submit to incarceration in the event of failure to repay a loan.

8

Getting Around

Highways, railways, and even rivers are all privately owned in Free America. Most roads have electronic toll systems, and your car should be equipped with a reader that can communicate with all of the systems in use. The cost per mile of the street you are driving on is displayed on a screen in your car, and the amount is immediately deducted from your bank account as you drive. Your reader will broadcast information about you and your protection firm; if you attempt to drive on a street when there are insufficient funds in your bank account, or if you do not have an account associated with your car's reading device, the road management company will contact your protection firm for payment.

If you drive on a road without a properly functioning reader, you will quickly be met by a security patrol. If you are unable to provide payment or information about your protection contract, they may impound your vehicle or even arrest you. The transition between roads owned by different companies is usually seamless, although vehicle standards can vary. For example, many communities have noise and pollution standards for cars. If you are driving a car that does not meet the standards of the road's owner, you will not be allowed to drive on it. Pollution certifications are usually programmed into your car's reading device, and are automatically passed on to the control system of the road on which you are driving.

The GPS system that allows vehicle monitoring was originally developed by the government of the united states, but is now operated by private companies. GPS devices are licensed by these companies, and they must have the proper codes entered into them to work, and the codes only work if payment has been received. World-wide revenue has been enough to allow these companies to launch new satellites and substantially improve services.

As you drive, you will find that you may enter some towns and cities and not others. Open cities have no checkpoints, and you can generally drive wherever you like; however, closed cities require permission to enter. If you have not purchased an entry permit, or if your application for a permit has been denied, you will not be allowed to pass the checkpoints at the edge of the city. Completely open and completely closed cities are now uncommon, with nearly all large cities at least excluding certain criminals. Some cities allow entry to everyone, but contain closed neighborhoods.

To apply for entry into a closed city or neighborhood, you should go to their website and enter your identifying information. Cities and neighborhoods often exclude those with criminal records, and some exclude anyone with a low income or net worth. Others exclude members of certain racial or ethnic groups and others exclude people based on age, sex, religion, or sexual preference. Always remember that property is private in Free America, and the owners of property have no obligation to share it with you.

The overland road system in Free America is essentially the same as it was in 2020. It is very difficult to construct new overland roads or widen existing roads, because property owners are resistant to selling land at a price that will allow profitable road operation. Entrepreneurs are responding by building a network of underground highways, which can now be built for less than ten million dollars per mile, and these roads have proven to be profitable with tolls as low as twenty cents per mile. It is now possible to drive across large parts of the country underground, with automatic vehicle control, allowing drivers to work or sleep while they travel.

Automatic vehicle control is also being installed on many overland highways as companies controlling different highway routes between cities compete for motorists. In large cities, road fees can increase dramatically during periods of high demand. After large sporting events, for example, road fees can be very high, encouraging some fans to wait until traffic clears before leaving. Under normal circumstances, however, tolls only need to rise by small amounts during peak travel times to convince enough people to postpone their trips to ensure that traffic continues moving smoothly.

The navigation system in your car can, in addition to computing the fastest or most scenic route to your destination, also calculates the cheapest route. On a long trip, you may be directed away from large cities, where roads are heavily used, and also away from scenic routes, which may have higher per-mile prices. Road prices are constantly changing, so sometimes your navigation system will ask you if you would like to change your route to take advantage of special deals. You can also specify a value of your time so that your navigation system can compute the route that minimizes the total of your time, fuel, and road toll costs.

9

Health and Medical Care

Anyone in Free America can say they are a doctor and see patients for money. Some medical practitioners have a great deal of training, and some have very little. Physicians with certification from the American Medical Association have received at least as much training as physicians in other countries that have government-licensed doctors. These physicians are, of course, more expensive than those with less training, but their costs have come down in recent years, as highly trained doctors from poorer countries have immigrated to Free America. For routine medical matters, such as advice about medications, simple tests, or minor complaints, doctors who are not AMA-certified are often satisfactory and cost far less.

Medical Insurance

Medical insurance is widely available in Free America, but policies with high deductibles are much less expensive than those with low or no deductibles. As a result, many people now pay all of their routine medical costs without help from insurance. Only the costs of rare and unpredictable events, such as injury or treatment for disease unpredicted by genetic tests, are generally paid by insurance companies. The costs of these policies vary considerably with the quality of care that is covered. Policies that reimburse AMA-certified care for all medical needs are not affordable for unskilled workers, for example. Those with low incomes purchase policies that will pay for lower-cost care. For example, a person with a broken leg might be sent to a bone setting specialist with little additional medical training. In the vast majority of cases, outcomes from this type of treatment are good, but in the event of significant complications, low-cost insurance coverage may provide inferior care.

Medical insurance companies all require an extensive battery of genetic and other tests before they will offer an insurance policy. The rate you pay for insurance will depend on the results of these tests. You may opt to exclude certain conditions from your coverage if you are unable to afford it. For example, if a genetic test finds that you are likely to develop Parkinson's disease, coverage would be quite expensive unless treatment for that condition was specifically excluded from your policy.

The Free American medical insurance system has had an interesting effect on the health of the immigrant population. Immigrants are overwhelmingly very healthy, since those with medical conditions know that they will be unable to obtain affordable insurance in Free America. As a result, healthy immigrants are usually able to obtain medical insurance coverage at very affordable prices. The effect of emigration of healthy people has also been felt in government-controlled countries around the world. As millions of healthy people move to Free America, those remaining behind are increasingly raising the costs of government-run health systems.

Much has been written about the "lost generation" of Free Americans with treatable conditions who have been unable to obtain medical care. It is certainly true that many people with known medical conditions before the introduction of long-term insurance plans have been unable to obtain high-quality treatment. This situation has improved significantly due to recent drops in medical costs, but many are still unable to afford medical care beyond questionable therapies offered by untrained medical practitioners. The tragedy of the "lost generation," however, has revolutionized insurance coverage for children. Seeing the dangers of being uncovered later in life, parents now routinely purchase long-term medical insurance for their children before they are conceived. These policies carry guarantees that coverage will not be dropped for any reason during the lifetime of the child, except in cases of nonpayment of premiums. Premiums are somewhat lower if policyholders agree to abortions in case a genetic predisposition to certain medical conditions is discovered before birth, but many who are opposed to abortion opt to pay the extra cost of policies without these provisions.

Most people of all ages without known medical conditions are able, if they choose, to purchase some acceptable level of long-term catastrophic insurance coverage. The coverage is unrelated to employment and area of residence, as medical insurance was before the collapse of the united states government. Many people take out additional insurance to make certain that their medical insurance premiums are paid. For example, job termination insurance is available that will pay medical insurance premiums for a short time in the event that the insured person loses employment. Medical insurance companies have taken steps to mitigate the risks to policyholders in the event of a bankruptcy of an insurance company, through agreements between firms to take on the policies of other companies in the event of their failure.

Alternative Medicine

A dizzying array of alternative medicine is flourishing in Free America. Drugstores stock "miracle cures" for every ailment, and storefront clinics offer every treatment from acupuncture to zinc therapy. Traditional physicians recognize that many of these treatments achieve some degree of success, but maintain that it is almost entirely due to the placebo effect—positive attitudes are healthy, so belief that a treatment will work sometimes improves health. Many patients do not appear to care whether this is the case, and they flock to alternative medical practitioners after reading stories of positive outcomes in advertisements. Many medical insurance companies offer policies that will only pay for practitioners in certain schools of thought.

Medical Malpractice

Protection firms are frequently involved in cases of medical malpractice, both with alternative and traditional practitioners. Some protection contracts protect against malpractice and promise to prosecute doctors who cause injury through negligent medical practice. All medical practitioners will verify your protection contract before offering treatment, and some will refuse treatment to those having contracts with protection firms known for taking action against physicians. Temporary waivers can be signed, but must be recorded with your protection firm to be valid, and this process can delay needed treatment in some circumstances.

There is a great deal of information about individual doctors, medical practitioners, hospitals, and medical insurance companies available on the Internet.

Overall Success of the Medical System

Although comprehensive nationwide data on mortality in Free America are not available, several studies of mortality have concluded that life expectancy continues to rise in Free America, once adjustments are made for the changing age and ethnic makeup of the country. While many in other countries find it difficult to believe, lowering the cost of basic medical care through the absence of regulation appears to have had a much more positive effect on overall health than any negative effect from the lack of regulation and government subsidy of medical care.

10

Intellectual Property

Attempts to implement some kind of generally accepted copyright and patent protection for authors and inventors in Free America have failed. Protection firms have tried to cooperate in the prosecution of copyright and patent infringement, both by defining intellectual works as property that can be stolen and by requiring strict contracts between buyers and sellers of intellectual works. In both cases, materials have been quickly sent to foreign countries to be copied, sold over the Internet, and shipped to individual purchasers in Free America. As it became clear that enforcement of intellectual property rights would be extremely expensive, protection firms declined to offer contracts to authors and inventors protecting their work. At the same time, Free Americans have pirated foreign intellectual works on an even more massive scale. Unauthorized copies of many foreign movies, books, video games, software, and branded consumer goods are available in stores and over the Internet at very low prices.

The lack of intellectual property protection in Free America has had many effects on the kinds of popular, professional, and scholarly work produced here. A few of these effects are described below.

Advertising

Advertising of various kinds finds its way into most publications in Free America. Display ads can be found in most books, and authors have found that if the advertisements are attractive, entertaining, and informative to readers, books are more valuable to readers with advertising than without it. Because scanning software can often distinguish display advertising from book text and illustrations, allowing copiers to delete them, authors try hard to make advertisements desirable so that pirates will copy them along with the book. The more a book's revenue comes from advertising that is pirated along with the book, the more an author welcomes unauthorized copying. In determining fees to be paid to authors, advertisers take account of potential exposure resulting from pirated editions.

"Product placement" is also increasingly common in books. Characters in books eat at restaurants that pay a fee to the author, and school textbooks contain math problems involving, for example, counting a particular brand of candy.

In certain works, the ubiquity of product placement has created a lack of trust of authors among readers. In these cases, protection firms have created contracts between authors and all potential readers, promising that payment has not been received by an author, either at all, or for particular aspects of a work. Any reader able to disprove this promise is entitled to a monetary reward.

Interactivity

Written words, images, and sounds can always be pirated. If human eyes can see it or human ears can hear it, a camera, scanner, or microphone can capture it, interpret the characters or words, and reproduce it. Interactive works, as simple as hyperlinked text or as complex as a virtual reality video game, are not as simple to copy because the code that controls them can be hidden. As a result, far more is published electronically with interactive enhancements in Free America than in other countries.

Many people believe that the increased interactivity of Free American art and literature has enlivened and improved it, while others believe that it has been cheapened with tricks and gimmicks. Whatever the case, Free American works are selling very well abroad, and many of the most popular artists and authors in the world now live and work in Free America.

Related to interactivity is the rebirth of movie theaters for the presentation of video productions. When piracy was suppressed by government, most filmmakers allowed their work to be streamed to homes over the Internet shortly after it was released, and so theater attendance declined. The turmoil of the early years of the century also convinced many families to stay home instead of venturing out to movie theaters. Rampant piracy of videos in recent years, however, has convinced many producers to switch to theater showings, where patrons can be carefully checked for recording devices to prevent surreptitious copies from being made.

Copy Protection

All anti-piracy technology is eventually overcome by hackers, but sometimes it takes a few years for them to succeed. The business of developing new and innovative anti-piracy software and devices is booming. Authors and artists often earn significant profits from the time a work is released until the time that the anti-piracy technology used is defeated.

Anti-piracy technology is similar to government copyright protection in that it provides a temporary monopoly to spur production, but eventually ends and gives the public the benefit of free access. The most popular works earn the highest profits quickly, but they are also the ones targeted by hackers the most frequently. Less popular and scholarly works often do not merit the same attention from hackers, and are sometimes able to prevent copying for a long period of time. Many economists believe that this kind of variable-length protection is superior to fixed-length government copyright protection in producing economically efficient outcomes.

Inventions

Without patent protection, the economics of research and development in Free America have changed significantly. Whole industries have moved abroad to take advantage of government patent protection that still exists in other countries, although their inventions are often quickly disassembled, copied, and reproduced by Free American engineers.

New drugs are often distributed directly to patients in order to avoid their being analyzed and copied by rival companies. Some rival companies initially hired patients to collect medication produced by their competitors and turn it over to them for analysis, but drug companies responded by hiring nurses to give patients daily injections of medications in their homes rather than risk pills falling into the wrong hands. The drug espionage war escalated when drug companies began paying these patients to analyze samples of their blood, which spawned a new area of research into the addition of compounds to medicines that would give false signals to analysts.

Last year, a pharmaceutical company took this effort to new heights by announcing that it had developed a drug that, if imperfectly copied, would likely poison anyone taking it. Research continues on drugs that, while effective against certain ailments, also produce side effects that only the inventing firm has the ability to cure. The side effects take time to develop and are different in different versions of the drug, so patients are afraid to take unauthorized versions of the drug.

The software industry has also developed elaborate defenses against copying. False code is inserted into most programs to throw off engineers who attempt to decompile and reverse-engineer them. Even "junk DNA" is inserted into newly invented biological organisms to confuse researchers from competing companies. It often takes several years for engineers to discover just how their competitors' new inventions actually work.

Employees of research and development companies are bound by strict contracts with their employers not to divulge trade secrets. Because the amounts of money involved can be very large, punishments for violating these contracts can be severe.

11

Children

As a parent, you are responsible for the education and protection of your children. You must inform your protection firm about any children you have or adopt, and add them to your protection contract. You should also obtain long-term medical insurance for your children before they are conceived to ensure that they have coverage before they develop any actual or predictable medical conditions.

Education

All schools in Free America are privately owned and are free to decide their own admissions policies, curricula, and tuitions. Education is completely voluntary, and many children are educated at home by their parents. Some schools are completely independent, while others belong to associations that require member institutions to adhere to certain standards. Schools compete fiercely for students, and many offer specialized courses and instruction. Some have very selective admission standards, while others will accept most students who are able to pay tuition. Some schools offer scholarships to promising students with limited financial means, while others do not.

Colleges and universities are flourishing in Free America, although the percentage of the population attending full-time programs is somewhat lower than it once was, probably because college attendance is no longer subsidized by state and federal governments. Loans are available for students to attend college, but it is common for lenders to demand a percentage of the borrower's salary for several years following graduation, in addition to minimum periodic payments.

Some companies are establishing trade schools to educate their future workers. Tuition is free, but students must sign contracts obligating them to work for the company for a period of time, usually four years. This arrangement is very similar to the training received by military officers for the united states government. In return for a free education, either at a government military academy or other college, cadets and midshipmen were legally obligated to undertake military service for several years after graduation.

Parent/Child Disputes

The question of the legal status of children has been a complicated issue in Free America. Parents pay for protection contracts and add their children to them; hence, the parent is the contract holder, not the child, so protection firms tend to side with parents in the event of a dispute. For example, runaway children are tracked down and returned to their parents by the parents' protection firm. Parents have been reluctant to sign contracts that limit their parental rights, so children calling protection firms for action to be taken against abusive parents have often received no assistance.

Instead of protection firms, the protection of abused children has fallen to neighborhood associations and owners of housing companies. Deed covenants and rental agreements for homes usually require residents to follow a set of rules established by a neighborhood or owner. In some neighborhoods, abusive behavior toward children is prohibited. Neighborhood rules sometimes require residents to submit to home inspections in the event that an owner or neighborhood council finds reason to suspect abuse. If evidence of abuse is found, residents can be required to move away.

By the age of sixteen, however, most protection firms will allow children to remove themselves from their parents' protection policies, whether or not the parents agree. At that point, the children can move out of their parents' homes and obtain employment and a protection contract of their own.

Child Labor

Child labor is common in many areas of Free America, particularly where many new immigrants reside. Working conditions are a matter that is negotiated between employers, parents, and their protection firms. Large scale boycotts against firms employing children have proven ineffective, and the practice has continued. In wealthier areas, however, child labor is far less common or nonexistent.

Rumors in foreign countries of "baby factories" feeding vast child labor plantations in Free America are false. Orphaned children under the age of three are far more valuable to adoption agencies than they are to any industry. In many cases, adoption agencies will pay parents to place their unwanted young children up for adoption, both in Free America and around the world. Orphaned and abandoned children who cannot be placed with families live in nonprofit orphanages supported by donors. Orphanages have become some of the most popular charities in Free America, and conditions inside them are carefully monitored by many donors.

Marriage

The absence of government means that marriage in Free America is no longer an official government institution. Many protection firms do offer to enforce marriage contracts. Standard marriage contracts provide for joint custody of children and the sharing of economic resources. Optional provisions include promises of sexual fidelity, economic support, sharing of household work, and a variety of other things. Most protection firms offer marriage contracts to homosexual couples, and others offer contracts to groups of people—most commonly, men marrying multiple women, but occasionally, women marrying multiple men, or even groups of many men and women. There are some neighborhoods that prohibit adultery, and these communities are often selective about the marriage contracts that they recognize as valid.

Abortion

Property deeds in many neighborhoods contain covenants prohibiting the use of land by abortion clinics. Protection contracts are difficult and expensive for abortion clinics to obtain in some areas. Most large cities, however, do have abortion clinics that are advertised on the Internet. The protection firms that offer coverage to clinics have been successful in preventing attacks, and the owners of surrounding streets do not allow protests or harassment of clients.

Anti-abortion groups have had no success convincing protection firms to take action to prevent abortions in general.

12

Drugs, Prostitution, Gambling, and Guns

There are, of course, no laws against vices in Free America, but they are strictly regulated in other ways. Neighborhood and roadway rules, protection contract terms, employment terms, and medical insurance provisions all limit activities that were once prohibited by government law.

Drugs

Free America has the best recreational drugs in the world. Freed from government regulation, pharmaceutical companies have pushed their most talented researchers to produce safe and effective drugs that produce a bewildering variety of effects. Drugs are available to enhance and suppress memory, sexual desire, gregariousness, and inhibition. There are drugs that will keep a person awake and alert for days with no sleep and minimal side effects. Other drugs mimic the effects of alcohol, marijuana, cocaine, heroin, and other drugs, with far fewer side effects.

While the use of these new drugs has increased spectacularly, many people in Free America believe that they are destructive, and seek out protection firms that discourage their use. Protection firms have a variety of provisions concerning recreational drug use. Some prohibit such use and impose regular drug testing on all clients with protection contracts. These firms believe that recreational drug use is a good predictor of criminal behavior and that contracts with drug users will increase their costs. Premiums for protection contracts that prohibit drug use tend to be lower than other contracts, if other provisions are similar.

Many neighborhoods also prohibit drug use. Some go so far as to prohibit alcohol and tobacco use, and many prohibit marijuana. Prohibitions of drugs such as cocaine, heroin, LSD, and many new drugs are common, at least in neighborhoods that attract families with children. Violation of neighborhood rules can result in fines and exclusion from the neighborhood, either by terminating lease agreements, or a forced sale of a residence. Some neighborhoods force offenders to sell their property to the neighborhood association at a substantial loss.

Possession of drugs and/or alcohol on streets, shopping malls, or other commercial property is often prohibited. Anyone caught selling or possessing drugs in these areas is usually expelled, and their names and identifying information are placed in a database. Employers, protection firms, schools, and insurance companies subscribe to these databases and will often refuse employment or services to people listed in them.

Medical insurance companies often have provisions in their contracts concerning the use of drugs, alcohol, and tobacco. Rates are lower for individuals who promise that they will not use these substances, and proof of violation of such a promise is grounds for denial of claims against the insurance company. Drug and alcohol testing is a routine part of most medical treatment that is covered by insurance, and the results are given to medical insurance companies. Many new drugs with fewer side effects, however, are increasingly permitted by medical insurance companies, with no penalties.

Employers are free to conduct drug tests as a condition of employment. You should never take a drug test for which you expect to receive a positive result, because your employer is likely to sell your results to a database firm. Unless you have an agreement with your employer that the results will remain confidential, the employer is free to disclose this information. If you demand a confidentiality agreement, the employer likely will assume that you believe the test could be positive and will not hire you anyway.

An increasing number of cities, however, contain neighborhoods where drug use is tolerated or even encouraged. Drugs that are illegal in other countries are freely available in these neighborhoods. It is important to remember, however, that future employers, lenders, and contractors may refuse to do business with you if an address in one of these neighborhoods shows up on a database. Many of these communities are thriving, however, and employers within these communities are very tolerant of drug use.

Prostitution

Prostitution, particularly street prostitution, is prohibited in many neighborhoods and commercial districts. Many cities, however, have commercial districts where street prostitution is open and legal. Houses of prostitution exist in most cities, although many neighborhoods exclude them. Small prostitution businesses operating out of homes are common, but violate the rules of many neighborhoods.

Prostitution arranged on the Internet and conducted in hotels and private homes is extremely common. Some prostitutes offer long-term contracts enforced by reputable protection firms. Some have complained that the line between marriage and prostitution has been blurred in Free America, with many young, relatively poor women contracting with wealthier men to provide exclusive sex, companionship, and household work in exchange for a salary. Many of these relationships produce children. Protection firms have been rapidly updating contracts to deal with issues that arise in these situations, such as child custody disputes.

Gambling

Gambling is very prevalent in Free America. Most retail stores have lottery and slot machines, betting booths are open at most sporting events, and other gambling activities are available on the Internet. Keep in mind that gambling debts are as enforceable as any other debt, and penalties for failing to pay can be serious.

Guns

Rules concerning guns vary considerably across Free America. Many neighborhoods prohibit gun ownership, as do a few large cities. Some of these cities have checkpoints at all entrances, and entering vehicles are searched for weapons. In most areas, however, gun ownership and possession are unrestricted. There are also many neighborhoods and towns that require every resident to maintain an operable firearm as a crime deterrent.

Heavy weapons, such as mortars, tanks, and bombs, are prohibited in most neighborhoods and cities.

13

The Environment and Energy Use

Environmental protection in Free America always takes place within the context of property rights. Pollution is considered to be a problem to the extent that it interferes with the property rights of others. Because all land, including rivers, streams, lakes, and wilderness, is privately owned, any act of pollution will affect a private property owner with a protection contract. Pollution of the air is considered an assault on any individual who breathes it and has adverse health consequences. Advanced molecular identification techniques allow exposure to chemicals released by specific companies to be determined. Because protection firms are responsible for protecting people and their property, they are deeply involved in disputes regarding environmental protection.

One of the great ironies of recent history was the attempt by the so-called global warming movement to use the government for environmental protection. In a roundabout way, this effort contributed to massive environmental degradation. When a majority of the public became convinced that the global warming scare had been a hoax designed to increase government power, they retaliated by voting for candidates who supported the wholesale elimination of environmental regulations. In the absence of established ownership of air, water, and scenic resources, the lack of regulation gave companies incentives to reduce their costs by ignoring the impact of their actions on others and pollute the air, water, and land.

Water Pollution

Before the collapse of federal and state governments, states were considered to hold all rivers and streams in trust for the public. Supreme Court decisions had held that states were required to hold these properties in perpetuity, and could not sell them. As a result, rivers and streams were not included in the mass auctions of state and federal property in the 2020s and 2030s. When these governments ceased to function in the 2040s, owners of land adjacent to waterways began to assert new property rights. Typically, an owner of both sides of a river would claim ownership of the entire river along his boundaries, while an owner along a single bank would claim ownership to the midpoint of the river.

During the 2040s, there were many disputes between upstream and downstream owners regarding water usage, pollution, and navigation. Arbitrators for protection firms upheld previous legal principles regarding water usage and applied strict standards of protection regarding pollution for downstream owners. Downstream owners successfully sued upstream polluters for damages, which in some cases ended upstream operations that were causing pollution, and in other cases, led to the purchase of pollution rights.

Because damages resulting from navigation were deemed to be trivial, river owners have never been ruled able to prevent reasonable river navigation. At first, small owners along large rivers such as the Mississippi sued to prevent dredging, which they maintained caused water pollution, and refused to sell pollution rights to companies doing dredging work for barge operators. Eventually, however, these owners found that their protection firms were unwilling to defend their ability to prevent dredging.

Most cities have several water supply companies, but they service neighborhoods instead of individual homes. When local governments collapsed, the water companies found themselves with monopolies and no regulator to restrain their prices. Worried about whether they would survive in the long run, many decided to raise water prices and reap as much revenue as they could in the short run.

Because streets were uncontrolled and unowned, homeowners hastily installed water pipes to reach competing water suppliers. Some pipes were bolted to streets, while others were buried next to sidewalks; in other cases, streets were jackhammered, pipes were installed, and the streets were crudely restored.

For a time in some cities, competing water suppliers sabotaged each other's pipes, and water supplies were interrupted. The process became more orderly when neighborhood associations and for-profit housing companies took ownership of streets, with the help of their protection firms, which needed control of streets to service their customers. Eventually, most neighborhoods reconfigured their water supply systems so that they could potentially be supplied by at least two water supply companies. As soon as that happened, water rates usually plummeted, and water quality improved.

Ownership of previously existing water pipes continues to be contested in some areas, but most of these cases have been settled or decided.

Air Pollution

Scientific research has demonstrated that there are health risks for many air pollutants such as sulfur oxides. In 2047, a large group of homeowners asked their protection firms to shut down a nearby coal plant that they demonstrated had raised sulfur dioxide levels in the air above their property. They claimed that this was a continuing assault on the homeowners and demanded cessation and compensation for past damages.

The protection firm of the company operating the coal plant initially defended the company, claiming that air pollution did not constitute assault. The two protection firms could not agree on an arbitrator in the case—an event that is now extremely rare but that used to be more common.

Seeing a profitable opportunity to represent homeowners across Free America, the homeowners' protection firm surrounded the plant with hundreds of well-armed security personnel and used a tank to breach the plant's security perimeter. During negotiations, the plant security team managed to obtain an antitank missile launcher by helicopter. The threat of the missile launcher convinced the homeowners' firm to withdraw the expensive tank, and a standoff continued for several days.

Homeowners throughout Free America joined the standoff, and some brought heavy weapons. Other industrial companies ignored the coal plant's pleas for assistance, and eventually, the coal plant's protection firm revoked its coverage, citing a contract clause limiting its liability in cases of armed insurrection. The coal plant was dismantled and rebuilt in a more remote location. After this incident, arbitrators have consistently ruled in favor of the victims of air pollution who are able to demonstrate significant risk of damages. There have been no more violent incidents of this kind.

National Parks and Other Scenic Areas

Shortly before the collapse of the federal government, a private trust was established by interior department officials, and all national parks, monuments, and federally owned wilderness areas that had not been previously auctioned were transferred to the trust. These officials attracted many private donations to the trust on the condition that it operate the parks in a manner substantially similar to the way they had been operated in the past, with the exception that entrance fees for park visitors could be raised. Current fees average fifty dollars per visitor. While visits have declined from nearly 300 million per year to approximately 100 million per year, the revenue of $5 billion per year is more than double the previous federal budget for park operations. The officials who initially organized the trust have earned enormous salaries and bonuses from the trust, and also own several businesses that provide services to the parks and to park visitors.

In some states, state parks were also transferred to trusts, but in other states, parkland was auctioned. Some has been developed as high-end residential property, and other former parks have been converted into amusement parks.

When governments first began to collapse, property owners in scenic areas feared that some of their neighbors might take advantage of the lack of zoning and control to develop their property in ways that would destroy the traditional character of these areas. Property owners formed associations and signed agreements limiting future development. During these years, holdouts were often dealt with harshly. Some property owners were compelled to sign agreements at gunpoint, while others were forcibly evicted and property transfer documents were allegedly forged. Owners of roadways that depended on scenic surroundings to attract travelers were particularly aggressive in organizing these kinds of associations.

Although many of these early property transfers and agreements were questionable, protection firms and arbitrators have been very reluctant to challenge them. Allegedly injured pro-development parties have had difficulty cooperating, and in most cases, their claims have quietly died away. As a result, many scenic areas in Free America are better protected than ever before.

Today, violators of scenic areas are dealt with in a somewhat more orderly manner. In one recent case, the owner of a mountaintop in a scenic area leased his land to a billboard company that erected a very large, brightly lit advertising sign. Neighbors cut power to the sign, and continued to cut it whenever it was restored by the billboard company. No deed covenants prohibited signage, and so the property owner asked his protection agency to station guards to prevent his neighbors from sabotaging the billboard. The protection firm, reasoning that the cost of security exceeded the rental value of the billboard, refused the request, citing a clause in the protection contract prohibiting "odious or obnoxious behavior" on the part of customers. The protection agency did assist the property owner in negotiating with his neighbors, however, and obtained a small settlement from them. The neighbors also agreed to add deed covenants to all of their properties, prohibiting similar disturbances in the future.

Endangered Species

Several private charitable groups use their resources to purchase habitats of animal and plant species considered to be endangered. While they have had some success, private landowners are under no obligation to protect endangered species on their property. Charitable groups regularly publicize losses of various species in their fundraising campaigns.

The movement of population to cities and the depopulation of many rural areas, however, have reduced development pressure in some areas and have apparently allowed the recovery of populations of some previously endangered species. New city developments such as Free City, Colorado, and Libertown, Pennsylvania, have encroached on areas that environmentalists consider fragile. When land values exceed the market value of wildlife, little can be done to protect it.

Energy

Contrary to the predictions of many early in this century, world supplies of petroleum are plentiful. The situation for Free America, however, is more difficult. Property owners have been successful in blocking their neighbors from developing oil and gas resources because of potential damage and pollution. Moreover, beachfront property owners have prevented offshore drilling for oil. As a result, domestic production of petroleum products has declined dramatically. At the same time, foreign countries hostile to Free America have blocked sales of petroleum. While Free American traders have often been very successful in bribing leaders of oil producing countries into allowing sales, petroleum users recognize the vulnerability of supplies and have been seeking alternatives.

Nuclear power companies have been purchasing sites, and suits brought by distant property owners have failed during arbitration. Electricity rates across Free America have been falling rapidly as an increasing number of nuclear plants have been built. A growing number of road and highway owners have been installing "smart-strips" that provide power, communications, and control to vehicles, allowing them to be driven automatically on longer trips, freeing drivers for other tasks, and allowing vehicles to be driven without the use of petroleum-based fuels. The savings in gasoline consumption are expected to eventually reduce Free America's vulnerability to petroleum supply disruption.

As electricity rates have fallen, the use of energy-conserving appliances has declined. Energy efficiency in buildings has also declined as heating has increasingly been converted to cheap electric power. Furthermore, sales of small fuel-cell generators have increased as insurance against electricity supply interruption.

14

The Economy

Overall statistics on the Free American economy are less comprehensive than they are in government-controlled countries. Statistics that are available, however, as well as evidence obtained by simply touring booming cities and new cities under construction, and the number of immigrants moving here, are convincing proofs that rapid economic growth is taking place.

Composition of the Economy

The main factors changing the composition of the economy are immigration, foreign trade, and construction. Immigrants moving to Free America come from very diverse backgrounds. While millions of unskilled workers come to Free America every year, many others are doctors, engineers, craftspeople, and other skilled workers. Immigration seems to come in waves by profession as people in foreign countries learn of opportunities and inform others in their fields. As they come, they drive down labor prices in their industry. For example, a wave of immigration of medical professionals in the mid 2040s caused the cost of medical services to plummet, reducing the need for automated and robotic procedures. Many manufacturers of automated medical devices went out of business, while the number of hospitals and drop-in medical clinics multiplied. While relative incomes of medical professionals fell, Free America as a whole benefited enormously, because high-quality medical care became inexpensive and easily available.

During the 2040s, foreign governments successfully prevented trade with Free America. As the strength of Free America and the futility of attempts to undermine it have become clearer, some governments have abandoned these attempts. Private naval forces protecting convoys of ships carrying imports and exports to countries that will accept them have also helped to discourage interference with Free America's foreign trade. The lack of tariffs and rapid economic growth in Free America have made it an ideal market for many foreign companies, and trade in many types of products and services is growing rapidly.

The rapid influx of immigrants, the establishment of new cities, and the remaking of old cities in the absence of government controls has caused a boom in the construction industry. Construction cranes fill the skies everywhere in Free America. While employment in construction is presently high, it is clear that the construction boom will have to come to an end at some point, and many of these workers will need to find other employment. How smoothly this transition will occur is one of the greatest uncertainties about the Free American economy.

Manufacturing represents a much larger percentage of economic activity in Free America than it did twenty years ago, largely because of cheap labor of immigrants, export demand, and embargoes that other countries have placed on the export of some manufactured goods to Free America. The financial sector is growing again, thanks to massive deposits into secret bank accounts to avoid foreign taxation. The financial sector was nearly wiped out with the collapse of the dollar in 2039, and had great difficulty before investors began to have confidence in the new kinds of financial institutions that developed in Free America. Mining and other heavy industrial activities are currently declining because of the difficulty in paying property owners who are affected by these operations for permission to pollute. The service sector of the economy is so vast that it is impossible to measure or estimate. Moreover, the lack of licensing, regulation, and taxation means that anyone can offer services of any kind for compensation. Hair styling, cleaning, food preparation, massage, sexual services, home repair, hauling, and other small service businesses operate in every neighborhood in Free America.

Macroeconomic Stability

The Free American economy has been remarkably free of any noticeable downturn for the past fifteen years. It is possible that this will change if the rates of immigration or construction activity slow, but many economists believe that the elimination of government has significantly reduced business cycle risk in Free America.

Because the Free American economy is extremely decentralized, it is much less vulnerable to shocks than it once was. Government policy once had a very large effect on the economy, and could change dramatically and unpredictably with elections. No single institution has anywhere near the influence that government used to have. Excessive credit expansion was behind many past boom and bust cycles, and the elimination of various government subsidies to the financial industry appears to have reduced systemic episodes of over-leverage.

The monetary system of Free America also apparently contributes to macroeconomic stability. This has been a surprise to many observers, since the system was not designed at all, but evolved quickly in what seemed, at the time, to be a chaotic process. Free American economists now believe that the federal reserve, skilled as its economists may have been, was incapable of adjusting monetary policy as quickly and accurately as unregulated market forces are able to do. In contrast to past descriptions of the federal reserve as a "maestro," or highly skilled orchestra conductor, Free American economic historians use analogies such as a bull in a china shop or a clumsy giant unable to thread a needle.

In free financial markets, hundreds of millions of participants each contribute a bit of information by buying or selling. Market prices are the combined estimate of all of this information, and are therefore the best possible estimates of value. Interest rates on loans, for example, balance the supply of savings and the demand for investment, and interest rates on different currencies balance the supply and demand for different kinds of money. Because these prices adjust continuously, producers of loans and currency adjust supply continuously, so big surprises and big mistakes are rare. When mistakes are made, they are confined to single institutions instead of affecting the entire economy.

By contrast, the federal reserve paid no interest on currency, and monopolized its production using "legal tender" laws. It attempted to direct the supply of other money, such as demand deposits, by manipulating the interest rate that the banks charged each other. Not being a profit-making institution, the fed had no pecuniary incentive to get things right and plenty of political incentive to act irresponsibly. Expert economists tried to make the right calls, but expert judgment is no substitute for collective wisdom, and professional expertise is no match for political ambition.

Errors by the fed were inevitable, given the constraints under which it operated, and they caused a great deal of economic distortion. These errors affected the entire economy, and there was no natural mechanism to counter them, so the fed's actions tended to cause imbalances to build up over time until recessions resulted, putting millions of people out of work. In less than a decade, innovation in response to competitive pressure on the part of suppliers of currency and other financial services has had the unexpected effect of eliminating macroeconomic problems that had troubled economists and government policymakers for over one hundred years.

Monopoly

Many commentators in recent years have predicted the growth of giant business monopolies in Free America. They believed that "trusts" of the kind that grew at the turn of the nineteenth and twentieth centuries would take over many industries, raise prices, produce low-quality goods, and strangle competition. Activities such as price-fixing, exclusive dealing, and attempts to monopolize or form cartels are not considered crimes in Free America, but the amount of competition in most businesses is shocking to many foreign observers.

Businesses in Free America do, of course, try however they can to gain market power and beat their competition. Violent methods, such as destroying a competitor's shop, are not allowed by protection firms, and all businesses, even the largest ones, depend on protection firms for basic security. Other methods of preventing competition have failed in most industries. Attempts to drive out competitors with low prices have simply led to the bankruptcy of the would-be monopolists, because challengers always appear after prices are increased. Cartels of firms have regularly broken down as members strike secret deals with customers at lower than cartel-sanctioned prices.

As the economy has become more competitive over time, it has become increasingly clear that anti-competitive practices were largely the result of government policies. Companies with political influence would lobby governments to take actions that hobbled their smaller competitors. These actions were always justified as forms of protection for the public, but their real purpose was to restrict competition and increase profits. Very few industries are now dominated by large firms.

Poverty

Free America has absorbed tens of millions of immigrants, many of whom had no assets and no occupational skills. As a result, the number of people considered poor in many Free American cities has increased in recent years. In some ways, their standard of living is lower than was the case for the poor in the government-controlled united states, since at that time, the poor were required to purchase higher quality housing, food, medical care, and vehicles than they might freely choose. More of the poor live in crowded, substandard housing than used to be the case; more of them eat food that is produced at a lower cost than used to be allowed; more visit medical practitioners with less training than used to be common; and more drive automobiles that are built to the standards of 120 years ago.

The poor, however, are able to live far more cheaply than they were allowed to live just twenty years ago. By choosing to live inexpensively, they are able to save and invest significant amounts of money. For example, families living on rice and beans in tiny apartments so that their children can attend the best schools are common. Other families send their children to work at young ages, pool their earnings, and build successful businesses. Others make the choice to live cheaply and work very little. While these families may not appear to wealthy people to be better off than they were under government control, most of them are at least pleased to be able to make their own decisions and are proud of what they hope to accomplish with their savings.

Charitable institutions continue to serve the poor, but their donations are increasingly coming from abroad. Foreign governments sponsor charity drives for the "starving in America" as part of their propaganda campaigns against Free America. As a result, Free Americans increasingly view these organizations with suspicion and have reduced their donations. With the abundance of "Hiring" signs in the windows of businesses, Free Americans are also skeptical of claims that the poor are unable to support themselves.

In most cities, poverty is not apparent to the majority of residents. Owners of most streets do not permit begging or vagrancy. Moreover, the owners of highways have found that traffic is better on roads without views of tenements, so most commuters and shoppers have never seen the poorer areas of their cities.

Investment

Investment opportunities are plentiful in Free America. Perhaps the biggest difference between investment here and investment in other countries is the fact that in Free America, businesses of any size are able to sell shares in public markets. Even single individuals often sell shares of their own future income on stock exchanges. While people and businesses are free to devise any contractual terms they would like with their shareholders, numerous stock exchanges around the country have developed standardized contracts that make it easier for investors to diversify their holdings of small businesses and individuals.

To take one small example, a laundromat in Dubuque, Iowa, recently sold a 10 percent stake in its business in order to raise money to purchase updated washers and dryers. Most of this new stock will be purchased by mutual funds, with final investors holding small pieces of thousands of different businesses. A monitoring firm employed by the stock exchange keeps track of the laundromat's receipts and expenditures, reporting this information to investors. If the laundromat pays regular dividends, its share price will rise, and future sales of shares will bring more cash.

Large stock exchanges, such as the New York Stock Exchange, have very strict standards regarding the disclosure of relevant information to investors, accounting, and stock price manipulation. Even on these exchanges, however, activities such as short selling and the creation of complex derivative securities are much freer than in other countries. On the many smaller stock exchanges throughout the country, financial innovation is rapid and uncontrolled. The cost of going public on these exchanges is very low, and firms with good reputations are able to raise large amounts of capital very cheaply.

Prices of securities are very high in Free America, meaning that average rates of return on investments can be very low. This is partly due to foreign investment that is pouring into Free America even faster than are immigrants. Foreign investors send money to Free America in order to avoid taxes in their own countries, exploiting the strict secrecy that Free American financial institutions offer. Another reason for high securities prices is the high savings rate of Free Americans, which is now the highest in the world.

Retirement

There are no government-guaranteed pensions in Free America, so it is very important that you plan for your retirement. It is unusual for employers to offer pensions; they simply pay market wages and assume that you will make arrangements to save appropriately for retirement. Since there are no taxes, there are no tax incentives for employers to offer fringe benefits such as pensions instead of cash.

Many investment companies will automatically deduct savings from your pay and place them in a set of investments. Some of these companies, such as Hard Rock Savings, are very reputable and have long records of success, but it is a good idea to diversify your savings with several investment companies.

15

Relations with Other Countries

Many countries around the world are hostile toward Free America. Watching the demise of a major government naturally gave other governments reason to worry. It is known that several governments have active programs to destabilize Free America in the hope that a traditional government can someday be reestablished.

This hostility has made many Free Americans highly suspicious of new immigrants. It is not advisable to express opinions that might be perceived as hostile to Free America, since employers might refuse to hire you and businesses might not transact with you. There are also committees of Free Americans who monitor what they consider to be subversive activities, and they publish databases of the people they consider to be potential spies and saboteurs.

Defense of Free America is a complex topic. The Free American Defense Committee still maintains the nuclear deterrent capability once managed by the armed forces of the united states government. The committee consists of former military officers and business leaders. Many businesses contribute funds to the committee, and they usually display an FADC sign at their retail locations. Many Free Americans refuse to do business with any firm that is not a member of the FADC, so many businesses consider membership a good investment.

Some large protection firms have developed limited military capabilities. Protection firms with shipping company clients have purchased former navy ships to escort convoys of their client's vessels, and some protection firms with clients located in border areas have obtained armored vehicles and heavy weapons. So-called "privateers" have retaliated against foreign naval ships that have attacked Free American shipping. Shipping protection firms that have lost ships to foreign attack have announced that they will purchase foreign ships that were involved in the attacks if they are captured. Privateers have devised creative attack strategies that have knocked out the command

and control systems of foreign ships and then captured them and sold them to the protection firms. When attacks on Free American shipping ceased, some former privateers shifted into outright piracy, preying on foreign ships delivering goods to Free American ports, mostly illegal shipping from countries that discouraged trade with Free America. In order to demonstrate to foreign countries that shipping to Free America was safe, a group of importers hired a protection firm to destroy a pirate base in the Virgin Islands. Piracy in the Western Hemisphere has since become much less common.

Trade bans that were imposed by many countries during the 2040s have mostly broken down, and foreign trade is flourishing, with the major exception of the purchase of foreign oil by Free America, which many governments are still trying to prevent.

16

The Future of Free America

It is impossible to know just how fast the Free American economy is growing, since there are no government statistics, and privately gathered statistics that are publicly available are nowhere near as comprehensive as government statistics used to be. Without tax returns, financial data on individuals and companies are not centrally available.

The pace of visible construction and development, the vigor and vitality of cities, and the massive influx of immigrants, however, suggest that the economy is booming. Unemployment appears to be rare, and homelessness is practically nonexistent, although this is partly because private street owners do not allow homeless people to loiter, and cheap tenements are plentiful. Churches and charity shelters advertising for donations report tremendous demand, but cities that ban these charitable activities do not seem to have any more problems with poverty than cities that do permit them.

The economy of Free America is more diverse than it was in the united states of America twenty years ago. Manufacturing, much of which had moved to other countries, has returned because the lack of taxes and unnecessary regulation has greatly lowered operating costs. Despite the fact that workers are moving to Free America to obtain higher overall living standards than they can obtain in their home countries, labor is now cheaper to hire and is more productive in Free America than anywhere in the world. This seeming paradox is explained by the lack of government intermediation in labor markets. Without the "middle man" of government, businesses save money, even as their workers are paid more. The one area where manufacturing costs are higher in Free America than in other countries is in environmental protection. Protection firms regard air pollution as a violation of property rights, and will prosecute factories that release dangerous quantities of pollution into the air. Because all rivers and streams are privately owned, property rights also prevent their contamination. Manufacturing activity that does not cause demonstrable harm by polluting, however, is growing rapidly and is producing low-cost, high-quality goods that are exported in huge quantities around the world.

Population, judging from the crowded flights and ships coming into Free America and the largely empty ones going out, is growing rapidly. On the crowded streets of open cities, a cacophony of languages and an amazing mixture of cooking smells stun the senses. At the same time, closed English-only cities are quiet and orderly, and appear to be maintaining their populations. Many rural areas have emptied out, or have had their populations replaced by immigrants.

America has also changed in more subtle ways over the past twenty years. The news is different, for example. News used to be dominated by the announcements of politicians and opinion pages focused on political questions. There are no more politicians and no more politics in Free America, so news tends to be less controversial. News headlines are usually about new products and services that are available, and essays and opinion pieces are often essentially advertisements for various communities. Among intellectuals, attention that used to be focused on politics and ideology is now concerned with literature, art, and higher philosophy. Among the general public, entertainment has become cheaper, more widely available, and more spectacular.

History is viewed differently than it used to be. united states presidents and other political figures, for example, receive much less attention than before. History textbooks increasingly focus on business leaders instead of politicians. Some people are nostalgic for the statist past, however, and they maintain some historical monuments that commemorate the united states government. While most presidential libraries have closed due to lack of visitors and funding, for example, the Franklin Roosevelt monument at Hyde Park, New York, has become a focal point for those who miss government, and the site has become very profitable.

In academics, there has been a shift away from the hard sciences and into the humanities and business. The hard sciences were heavily subsidized by the old united states government, partly through direct government grants, and indirectly through patent protection. Now that both of these are gone, a great deal of the basic scientific research that used to be conducted here has shifted to other countries, with useful results copied (either openly or through industrial espionage) for use by businesses in Free America. Students who once would have studied the physical sciences now study engineering, business, and the humanities. Salaries for doctors have fallen because of competition from immigrants, so fewer native-born Free Americans are studying medicine.

Religion is alive and well in Free America, although it is changing rapidly. Religious organizations used to be careful to preserve their exemptions from property and income taxes by avoiding certain commercial activities and the appearance of earning profits. Churches are now under no such scrutiny, and many operate huge conglomerate businesses. The line between religion and business is becoming increasingly blurred as organizations offer spiritual instruction, worship services, and charitable aid in addition to conventional business products, particularly insurance, real estate development and brokerage, financial planning, and management consulting. New religions roughly based on ancient Gnosticism are growing particularly rapidly. These groups' believe in a less centralized deity than traditional Christianity, Judaism, and Islam, and their belief that sparks of divinity reside in some people appeals to Free Americans living in a decentralized society. Polytheistic religions are also growing in some areas.

Many Free Americans now believe that politics had poisoned the atmosphere of the country before the collapse of government. Voting, once considered a sacred aspect of political freedom, is now considered by many to be a symbol of divisiveness and unproductive conflict. While some large businesses are publicly owned and have voting shares, and some homeowner associations resolve certain questions by voting, most businesses are now largely privately held or controlled by relatively few investment funds, with the public holding nonvoting shares, and most neighborhoods are now owned and controlled by for-profit housing companies instead of homeowner associations.

It is often observed that reputation is of primary importance in Free America, much more so than in government-controlled countries. Reputations are easy to gauge, since several websites offer dossiers and business histories of nearly every person in Free America. Individuals with poor reputations have great difficulty finding companies that are willing to sign long-term contracts at reasonable rates. As a result, education that stresses virtue, ethics, and morality is becoming more popular. Conduct and even dress that is taken to signal virtue is spreading in many areas, with temperance societies and formal dress becoming prominent in some cities. Of course, there are many other areas where normal dress is extremely informal, and others where nudism is the norm. But in the central business districts of large cities, dress and manners seem somehow closer to those of the early twentieth century than to the early twenty-first century.

Free America is fragmented, with some communities completely cut off from the rest of the country, and others pursuing unique dreams and philosophies. There is a growing sense, however, that Free Americans have one thing in common—a belief in liberty as an ultimate good. The more esoteric various communities become, the more they depend on freedom from outside interference to maintain their lifestyles and beliefs. While many communities detest each other's lifestyles, they are united in their appreciation of the freedom they have to live as they desire. In "mainstream" communities throughout Free America, the pursuit of economic profit has become a dominant goal, and these people also appreciate the liberty they enjoy in Free America. Doing business without taxes and government regulations has proven so rewarding, so stimulating, and so productive that most Free American businesspeople can no longer imagine any other life. Government, once accepted as necessary for society to function, has lost all legitimacy in the minds of Free Americans, and libertarian ideas are spreading rapidly around the world.

Foreign governments continue to hold out hope that some sort of revolution will reestablish government in America. Most Free Americans do not believe that this is possible. Revolutions usually succeed by capturing centers of authority and using them to operate intact governmental institutions. The decentralized nature of Free America means that there is nothing useful for revolutionaries to capture. Attacks on individual businesses would be repulsed by protection firms. An attempt to simply proclaim a government would be met with the same laughter that would have occurred if an American of the early nineteenth century had proclaimed himself king. Free Americans no longer accept the authority of government, and reestablishing that acceptance appears to be impossible.

Index

25th Amendment to constitution, 7
Abortion, 69
Academics, 92–93
Advertising, 63–64
Air pollution, 77
Alternative medicine, 61
America, history and concept, 1
Anti-foreign-trade laws, 7
Anti-piracy technology, 65, *See* also Copy protection
Asset prices, 6
Association of Free America Protection Firms (AFAPF), 33
Borrowing, 2, *See* also Economy
   economic situation, 3
Capital punishment, 46
Certificates, 52
Charitable protection firms, 36–37
Child labor, 68–69
Communities, 25–26, 94
Company towns, 29
Contractual employment, 19–20
Convention, constitutional, 5
Copy protection, 65
Crises of 2020s and 2030s, 11
Cross of Gold speech, 3
Debt contracts, 46
Dollar-denominated bonds, 9
Drugs, 71–72
Economy
   composition of, 81–82
   investment opportunities, 85–86
   macroeconomic stability, 82–84
   monopoly, 84

    of Free America, 91
    poverty, 84–85
    retirement, 86
Education, 67–68
Employment disputes, 20
Endangered species, 79
Energy sources, 79–80
Environmental protection in Free America, 75–80
Federal debt ceiling, 3
Federal invasions of Mississippi and Oklahoma, 5
Financing methods, 2
Foreign invasion, 9–10
Foreign trade, 90
Free America
    cases, 40–44
    children, education and protection, 67–69
    communication, 55–57
    communities in, 23
    company towns, 29
    concept, 1
    contractual employment, 19–20
    copyright and patent infringement, 63–66
    development of cities, 23–25
    drugs, 71–73
    economy, 81–87
    employee and entrepreneur, 18
    employment disputes, 20
    environmental protection in, 75–80
    future of, 91–95
    health and medical care, 59–62
    housing quality, 28–29
    immigrants, 19
    income securitization, 20–21
    inflation and, 49–53
    jobs in, 17
    political cities, 26–28
    practical advice, 29
    protection, 31–40
    punishment in, 45–48
    relations with other countries, 89–90

skilled workers, 17–18
standard of living, 17
towns and neighborhoods in, 25–26
Free America Clean Eatery (FACE) sign, 14
Free American Defense Committee, 89
Free market institution-building, 10
Gambling, 73
General Security, 34
Gold certificate-issuing company, 10
Government borrowing, 2
Government-guaranteed pensions, 86
Guards and patrols, 36
Hard money political movement, 3
Hard Rock Savings, 87
Highway robberies, 4
Immigrant complex, 13
   business and shopping areas, 14–15
   criminal activity within, 14
Immigrants, criminal, 10
Immigration
   influx of immigrants, 82
   skilled workers, 81
   waves, 11
Incarceration firms, 47
Income securitization, 20–21
Inflation, 7
   memories of 1970, 3
Interactivity of Free American art and literature, 64
International Brotherhood of Teamsters, 18
Interstate 55 group, 4
Inventions, 65
Investors
   federal assets, 6
   government bonds, 2–3
   tax revenue, 2
Marriage, 69
Medical insurance, 59–61
Medical malpractice, 61
Mexican nationals from anti-foreigner riots, 9
Military government, 8

Minimum wage laws, 11
Money Honey, currency issue, 51–52
Mortality data, 61–62
National parks, 77–79
New York Stock Exchange, 86
Nuclear strikes of 2041, 11
Old Gold firm and certificates, 49–50
Parent/child disputes, 68
Political cities, 26–28
Politics and issues, 92
Population, 92
Presidential succession act, 8
Prison and living conditions, 45–46
Privateers, 89–90
Prostitution, 72–73
Protection
   cooperation between firms, 38–39
   firms, 36, 38–40
   levels, 31–33
Protection contract, 31–33
   cost, 37–38
   with General Security, 34
Public employee unions, 6
Reform party, electoral sucess, 2
Religion, 93
Repayment contracts, 15
Secretary of defense, 8
Shipping protection firms, 89–90
Slavery, 47
Sparked movements, 4
Spending programs, 3
   crime, 4
Strike wave, 7
Tax pledges, 1–2
Taxation, 2, *See also* Economy
   federal debt, 2–3
   political movements, 4
   state and local governments collapsed, 10
Third-party incarceration firm, 35
Towns and neighborhoods in Free America, 25–26

Trade, 90
Unemployment, 5
Unions, 6
Wages for jobs, 17–18
Water pollution, 75–77
Weapons, 73
White House security, 7

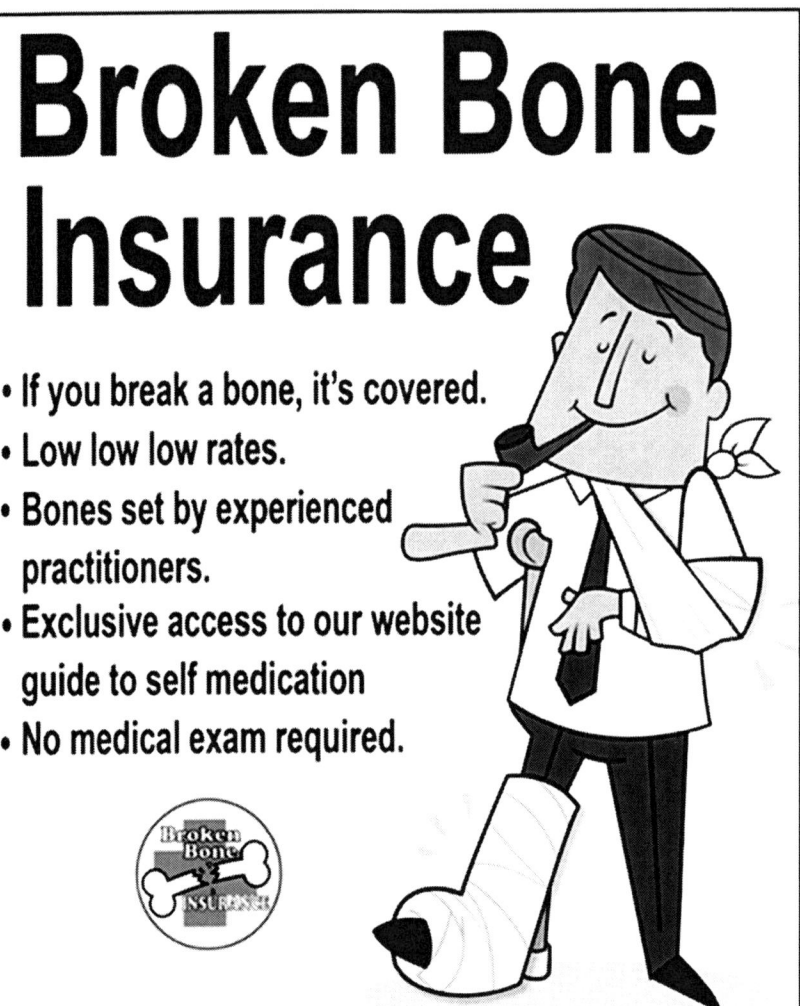

PROTECT YOUR FAMILY

By Contracting with All Safe

- Harshest punishments of any protection firm in Free America.

- Full Coverage alarms for your home.

- Constant video surveillance.

- Guaranteed armed response in 5 minutes.

- Significant discounts for personal GPS recording.

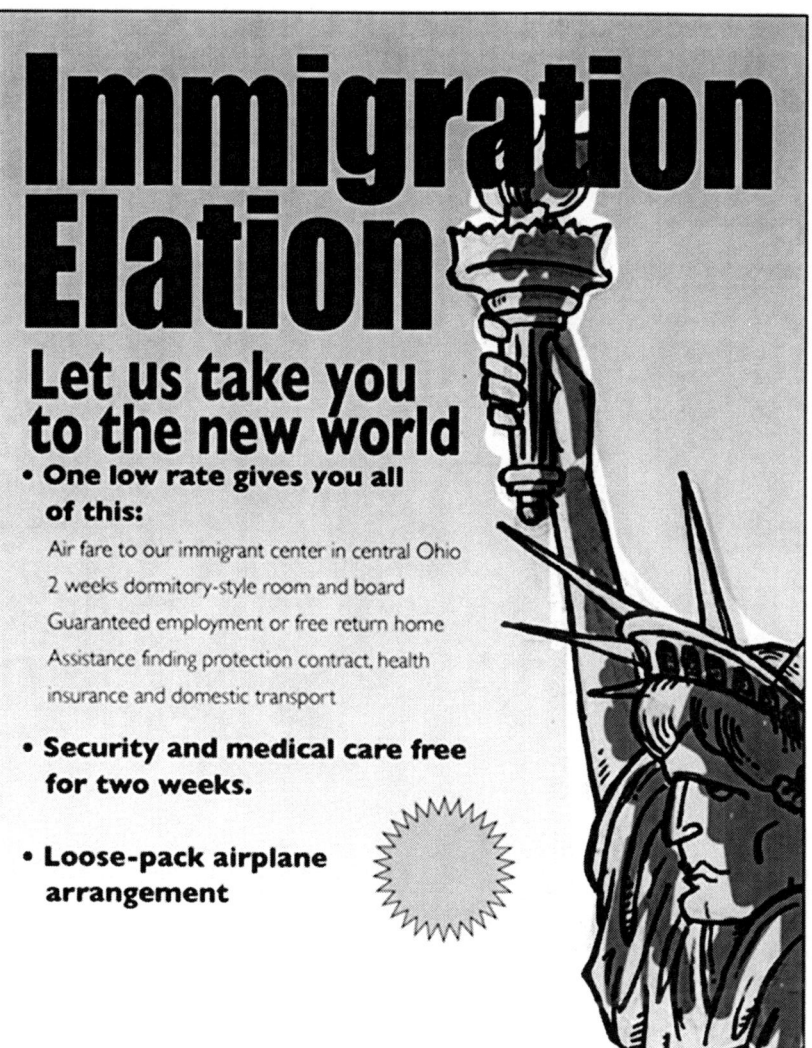

CPSIA information can be obtained at www.ICGtesting.com
Printed in the USA
BVOW05s1845070814

362078BV00003B/216/P